Kristen Suzanne's
EASY Raw Vegan Dehydrating

OTHER BOOKS BY KRISTEN SUZANNE

Kristen's Raw: The EASY Way to Get Started & Succeed at the Raw Food Vegan Diet & Lifestyle

Kristen Suzanne's EASY Raw Vegan Entrees

Kristen Suzanne's EASY Raw Vegan Desserts

Kristen Suzanne's EASY Raw Vegan Soups

Kristen Suzanne's EASY Raw Vegan Sides & Snacks

Kristen Suzanne's EASY Raw Vegan Salads & Dressings

Kristen Suzanne's EASY Raw Vegan Smoothies, Juices, Elixirs & Drinks (includes wine drinks!)

Kristen Suzanne's EASY Raw Vegan Holidays

Kristen Suzanne's Ultimate Raw Vegan Hemp Recipes

Kristen Suzanne's Ultimate Raw Vegan Chocolate Recipes

Kristen Suzanne's EASY Raw Vegan Transition Recipes

For details, Raw Food resources, and Kristen's free
Raw Food newsletter, please visit:

KristensRaw.com

Kristen Suzanne's

EASY Raw Vegan Dehydrating

Delicious & Easy Raw Food Recipes
for Dehydrating Fruits, Vegetables,
Nuts, Seeds, Pancakes, Crackers, Bread,
Granola, Bars & Wraps

by Kristen Suzanne

*Green
Butterfly
Press*

Scottsdale, Arizona

For information on excerpting, reprinting or licensing portions of this book, please write to info@greenbutterflypress.com.

Green Butterfly Press
19550 N. Gray Hawk Drive, Suite 1042
Scottsdale, AZ 85255 USA

Library of Congress Control Number: 2009920146
Library of Congress Subject Heading:
1. Cookery (Natural foods) 2. Raw foods

ISBN: 978-0-9817556-8-7

2.0

Contents

• • • • • • • •

5: Special Dehydrated Ingredients   61

Appendix A: Raw Basics   73

Appendix B: Resources   105

Recipe List

• • • • • • • • • •

1
· · ·

Dehydrating Fundamentals

Every human being is the author of his own health or disease.

THE BUDDHA

Dehydrating some of your raw food is a great aspect to the raw vegan lifestyle, because it adds variety, as well as shelf life. With a dehydrator, you can have crunchy foods, warm foods, marinated foods with a texture reminiscent of cooked food, and foods that can last a long time in your pantry, refrigerator or freezer. One of the biggest challenges people think they'll encounter with raw food cuisine is *not having enough time* to prepare the food and/or not having enough variety. Bringing a dehydrator into your life solves both of these issues.

WHAT IS DEHYDRATING AND HOW DOES IT WORK?

Dehydrating your raw food at a low temperature is a technique that warms and dries your food while preserving its nutritional integrity. You are removing moisture from the food so bacteria, yeast and mold don't grow and spoil the food. The food becomes lighter in weight because the water weight is gone.

This is great for the raw food lifestyle because you can make something and eat it at a later date. You don't always have to eat everything immediately after you make it. This can make life much easier, especially when you're new to Raw.

Dehydrating your food is really simple. You'll find some great recipes to get you started in this book. This style of preparing food offers you the opportunity to enjoy foods that are crunchy like crackers and vegetable chips, as well as chewy and pliable like fruit leather. You can always have something delicious on hand when you are hungry; this is especially helpful when you find yourself strapped for time and needing something fast. Dehydrating is useful for food preparation that you need to do in advance. For example, if you know you're going to be entertaining next month, you can start some of the preparations right now by making your breads and crackers ahead of time.

When you use a dehydrator you can also save a lot of money. I find myself easily saving money when I make my own dehydrated foods as opposed to buying pre-dried, packaged foods.

WHAT KIND OF DEHYDRATOR SHOULD I GET?

There are many brands on the market, but there is only one that I truly love. My favorite is from Excalibur because they are trusted, their technology is state of the art (as well as their customer service), and they have something for everyone. They have been the leaders in dehydration technology for over 35 years. If you ask around among raw fooders and people in-the-know, you'll almost always find that Excalibur is the name most recommended.

Excalibur offers dehydrators in several different sizes and all I can truthfully say... "bigger is better." So often I hear from clients of mine that they bought the 5-tray version instead of the 9-tray model, and they wished they had gone with the bigger choice. They thought they wouldn't need all 9 trays... but realized that they indeed should have gone bigger. Dehydrating is so easy and fun that you'll find yourself doing it frequently. With the 5-tray version, you'll run out of dehydrating space very quickly.

Excalibur products are designed to be environmentally sound, so when you purchase an Excalibur dehydrator, you are helping to maintain a cleaner, greener planet. Excalibur dehydrators' door, case, trays, and knobs are made from medical-grade recycled plastics. Furthermore, Excalibur dehydrators are designed to run on lower wattage thus saving electricity.

Through special arrangement, as a reader of my books, you can receive a 10% discount on all Excalibur products when you buy direct from the manufacturer by calling them, using the following information:

10% OFF EXCALIBUR DEHYDRATORS & PRODUCTS

**To receive your 10% discount,
order via toll-free number by calling:**

1-800-875-4254 Ext. 102

*Mention the
"Kristen's Raw 10% Discount"*

**For Excalibur product details, visit:
www.drying123.com**

Happy dehydrating!

SHOULD I GET A PLASTIC OR STAINLESS STEEL DEHYDRATOR?

According to Excalibur's expert staff:

> As stainless steel appliances have come into fashion one question remains: Is stainless steel better than plastic for food dehydration? Well it depends — not all stainless steel is created equal just like not all plastics are the same. Some people are under the misconception that stainless steel is healthier and of higher quality than plastic. However, it all depends on the grade of stainless steel. Lower grades of stainless steel can be mixed with other metals, which can change in color, density and safety when coming into contact with heat and food.
>
> When looking at a stainless steel dehydrator, here are the questions you MUST ask when it comes to your health and safety:
>
> - *What type of stainless steel is the dehydrator made out of?* Not all stainless steel is the same. To make stainless cheaper, typically lower grades are mixed with other metals, which can change the color, density and safety when coming into contact with heat and food.
>
> - *What are the trays made of?* Many low-grade stainless steel dehydrators do not come with stainless steel trays — they are sold with trays that are chrome plated and/or nickel-plated. Keep in mind your food is setting on these trays. Over time this plating can chip off in your food and rust. Chrome plating usually makes use of hexavalent chromium ($Cr+6$). Many studies in the last decade have shown it to be dangerous, citing evidence that hexavalent chromium

causes lung cancer and other serious health conditions. Because of these health concerns, the chrome plating process has come under increased regulations in the U.S. based on chrome's hazardous and environmentally toxic properties. In order to avoid increased regulations many companies have moved their operations overseas. Important: If you purchase a stainless steel dehydrator, make sure the trays are 100% stainless steel.

- *Where is the dehydrator manufactured?* Beware of low-grade stainless steel coming out of China (and chrome plated trays from overseas). You can be proud buying your dehydrator from Excalibur, because it is a U.S. made product.

- *Is the dehydrator a green product?* Stainless steel is not green. Although, it is a necessity in commercial applications, it is not needed for home use dehydrators. Support green products, buy recycled, and Buy Green!

- *How long has the manufacturer been in business and what is the warranty?* Beware of companies that purchase low-grade dehydrators from China and put their name on it. Parts might not be available when needed and many of them cook foods rather than dehydrate them.

- *Are the edges rounded and seamless for easy cleaning?* Low-grade units will have sharp 90-degree corners and have cracks/crevices where the metal comes together. This is where food can become lodged creating the perfect environment for mold and bacteria to grow.

EXTRAS FOR YOUR DEHYDRATOR

There are a few extra tools for your dehydrator that you should also get to ensure the optimal dehydrating experience. Some dehydrator models come with these automatically, and some you have to buy as extras. Either way, you'll be very happy that you have them.

Timer

Life is much easier when your dehydrator has a timer. This is a great tool because the dehydrator turns off when you schedule it. There have been many times I had to set my alarm clock for crazy hours during the night so I would wake up and turn it off. Life is much nicer when this is done automatically. Something to know... for people who forget to set the timer... if you dehydrate your food "too long" (i.e., it's too dry) then you can spritz it gently with water and bring it back from being too dry. Then, dehydrate it again until you attain your desired texture (if necessary).

Thermometer

This is an important tool to ensure you keep the temperature at a level that maintains the integrity of the nutrition. The dehydrator has a dial that you use to set the temperature of your dehydrator, but it doesn't always allow for setting an exact temperature. So, I take an extra precaution and stick a thermometer inside to ensure it's right where I want the temperature. The one I use is a *Taylor Digital Thermometer* that allows me to measure the temperature in the dehydrator without opening the door of the appliance.

ParaFlexx™ Premium Non-stick Dehydrator Sheets

These are a must if you want to maximize the use of your dehydrator. The Excalibur dehydrator comes with mesh sheets for the plastic trays. These mesh sheets are great for dehydrating foods that aren't too "wet," but they are hard to use when dehydrating something that has a batter consistency (or has a lot of water in it) such as pancakes, flax crackers, breads, and fruit leathers. This is where the ParaFlexx Premium non-stick sheets are required. ParaFlexx sheets are typically used for the first few hours of dehydrating, then you flip the food over onto the basic mesh screen (with holes for better ventilation), peel off the ParaFlexx non-stick sheet and continue drying your food until it's dehydrated thoroughly. Make sure you get enough sheets so you have one for each tray.

The sheets come in two varieties: disposable and non-disposable. The disposable sheets are convenient because you don't have to wash them, but over time, they add up in cost. The non-disposable sheets are simple to clean and prevent waste by not throwing them out. They last a long time. I'm still using the originals that I bought with my dehydrator years ago. If you don't have the ParaFlexx sheets, you can use unbleached parchment paper in place of them. They're not as "user-friendly" but they do work.

WHERE DO I KEEP MY DEHYDRATOR?

There are many places where you can store and/or use your dehydrator. It's typically *not* the smallest of your kitchen appliances and it can take up counter space. Excalibur's 9-tray dehydrator measures approximately 16.5"w × 12"h × 19"d. Furthermore, it's also not the kind of appliance that you want to take out of the cupboard every time you use it. I doubt that it will even fit in your cupboard. So, it's nice to find a place for it in your house and keep it there. The machine is very quiet... just a nice soft hum is all you hear. It does give off a little heat, so if you're in a warm climate like I am in Arizona, you might not want it in a part of the house that you're in a lot of the time during the summer. Therefore, my dehydrator found a great home on top of my dryer in the laundry room. My mom keeps hers in her dining room, since she doesn't use that room very often. And, my friend keeps his in the kitchen. Some people keep it in the garage or on the patio. You can keep it pretty much anywhere... don't think it belongs only in the kitchen if you're limited in space there.

Using your dehydrator is one of the easiest machines to operate in the world. All you have to do is make a simple recipe, put it in the dehydrator and let it work its magic. Simple.

PROPER DEHYDRATION TECHNIQUES

Most dehydrated foods result in a pliable texture (almost chewy) and they tend to be darker in color and sweeter in taste because they're more concentrated than they were prior to drying. Here's a tip... if you want to grind a dehydrated food into a powder, such as sun-dried tomatoes but the tomatoes are too pliable to grind, put them in the freezer for a couple hours. They are easier to break and grind when they're frozen.

Some people like to use a "dipping solution" before dehydrating their fruits and vegetables to help preserve the natural colors, as well as adding a little more flavor. Here are some to try: fresh lemon or lime juice work great with vegetables, and pineapple or orange juice are nice for fruits... or vice versa. You can also use two tablespoons of fresh juice mixed with one cup of water. Then, simply dip the fruit or vegetable and dehydrate.

You can also change the look of what you're dehydrating by dipping the fruit or vegetable in something that has a dark color to it. For example, cranberry juice is fun for dipping. Dip pineapple or apple slices in cranberry juice or jicama or cauliflower in beet juice. Then, simply dehydrate. It's fun and very pretty.

TEMPERATURES

When using an Excalibur dehydrator, it's recommended that you begin the dehydrating process at a temperature of about 140 degrees F for 1–2 hours. Then, lower the temperature to 105–115 degrees F for the remaining time of dehydration. Using a high temperature such as 140 degrees F, *in the initial stages of dehydration*, does not destroy the nutritional value of the food because it's during this initial phase that the food does the most "sweating" (releasing moisture). When this occurs, it is cooling the food. Therefore, while the temperature of the air circulating *around* the food is about 140 degrees F, the food itself is actually cooler. These directions apply only when using an Excalibur Dehydrator, because of the Horizontal-Airflow Drying System.

DO I USE STAINLESS STEEL OR GLASS BOWLS/ PLATES WHEN USING MY DEHYDRATOR?

Never use a stainless steel or metal dish with your dehydrator because it conducts heat. The dish will get quite hot, too hot to touch, which means it could be adding more heat to your food than you want. If I'm marinating some mushrooms or zucchini, for example, I will use a glass bowl or a glass mason jar in my dehydrator, and it works great. I do the same when warming my soups by using a glass mason jar.

CAN I DEHYDRATE BOTH SWEET AND SAVORY FOODS AT THE SAME TIME?

Yes, you can dehydrate both sweet and savory flavored foods at the same time. The flavors will not combine even if they're on the same tray.

IS IT POSSIBLE TO DEHYDRATE FOOD TOO LONG?

Not to worry; if the texture of your food gets too dry, simply mist it with purified water to reconstitute it. At that point, you can decide if you need to put it back in the dehydrator for a little while or not.

CUTTING AND SLICING TECHNIQUES

Slice your fruit or vegetables, using a knife, mandoline, or V-slicer, into desired thickness and shapes. I typically cut mine into ¼–½-inch thick pieces (thicker for watermelon, about 1-inch, since most of watermelon is just water, and there won't be much there after dehydration if you slice it too thin). It's best to try and keep a uniform thickness so they dehydrate at the same rate. The thicker you cut your fresh produce, the longer it'll take to dehydrate.

STORAGE FOR FOOD AFTER DEHYDRATING

You should store your dehydrated food in glass containers when possible, which seal tightly. I love using wide-mouth glass mason jars, which you can find at most grocery stores, hardware stores and online through my website at *KristensRaw.com/store*.

Glass is truly the healthiest option you can choose, and it's the most environmentally friendly. Using glass jars is also nice because you can easily see the contents. Depending on the food, most dehydrated foods will typically keep in the refrigerator for about 3–6 months, or up to a year in the freezer. Label your goodies by writing on the glass jar with a Sharpie™ marker (it comes off easily with a sponge and soapy water).

FANTASTIC THINGS YOU CAN DO WITH YOUR DEHYDRATOR

You can dehydrate most any fruit, vegetable, herb, edible flower (or decorative flowers), nuts, seeds, or whatever else your creative mind comes up with. Have fun!

Dehydrating Foods (of Course)

Virtually all Raw foods can be dehydrated, including fruits, vegetables, breads, crackers, nuts, and seeds. I love making my own sun-dried tomatoes by slicing fresh tomatoes thinly and placing them in the dehydrator. There are plenty of recipes to get you started in the pages that follow.

Adding Shelf Life

Storing foods for the winter months is definitely an age-old tradition, and doing so today accomplishes the same thing... only we do it year round. This is one of the ways to increase variety in your diet all year long, thus, maintaining balance in your diet. There are times in the winter that I'm craving berries (these are primarily available in the summer); therefore, I dehydrate them during the summer when they're at their peak for ripeness and nutrition, then I can enjoy them in the winter months, too.

Saving Money!

Don't throw your food scraps away. Dehydrate them. You can puree leftovers, in your blender or food processor, and make delicious plant leather (see Chapter 3). Or you can try dehydrating them for reconstituting at a later date.

Buy fresh, delicious seasonal produce, when it is less expensive. Dehydrate and store it so you can enjoy it all year long. You can eat the food in the dehydrated state or reconstitute it by soaking the food in water before consuming it.

Warming Foods

Dehydrators are very useful for warming Raw vegan foods, while still maintaining the integrity of the nutrients. This is particularly helpful in the winter months when you want something nice, comforting and warm. Put the food you want warmed in the dehydrator for 1–2 hours set at 125–130 degrees F. This is also particularly helpful for people who are new to Raw and don't always want to eat cold or room temperature foods.

Marinating Foods

Dehydrators are fantastic because they accelerate the marinating time of vegetables. Dehydrating softens them, intensifies their flavors and creates a cooked texture. Sometimes when I make a hearty, chopped veggie-filled soup, I'll put it in the dehydrator for a couple of hours and this helps soften some of the harder vegetables... things like carrots and beets. Flavors also become more intense and delicious. (Plus, it warms it up a bit—yum!)

Making Sauces

I use my dehydrator to thicken sauces, while preserving the nutritional value. In traditional cooking, simmering is used and called a "reduction" because the liquid evaporates—but the high heat destroys much of the nutritional value.

Adding Extra Nutrition to Other Foods

You can add extra nutrition into your recipes with your dehydrator. Pick out some nutrient dense foods, such as carrots, beets, zucchini skins, etc., then slice and dehydrate them completely. Grind them to a powder and store in a glass mason jar in your refrigerator. The next time you make a smoothie, soup or salad, add some of this high nutrient dense powder to your recipe and feel your body's cells loving all that extra nutrition.

2
...

Fruits & Veggies

It is health that is real wealth and not pieces of gold and silver.

MAHATMA GANDHI

This is simple and delicious. Take any fruit or vegetable that you want to give a longer shelf life to, or for anything of which you want a more concentrated flavor, and dehydrate it. Slice the fruit or vegetable, lay the slices in a single layer on the mesh dehydrator sheet and dehydrate until thoroughly dry.

See photo at KristensRaw.com/photos.

The thinner you slice them, the faster they will dehydrate. One of my favorite ways to eat dehydrated fruits and veggies is when they're *partially* dehydrated. They're still juicy, but have some warmth to them. So, next time you are dehydrating your produce, sneak a few pieces to snack on while they're dehydrating and enjoy a real treat! But, watch out! You might find you and your family eating them all! (*Note: When dehydrating, use only ripe produce for best results.*)

For more fun and variety, sprinkle your fruits and vegetables with different seasonings. I like putting cinnamon on my banana slices and I like sprinkling garlic or onion powder on my zucchini slices. Sliced pineapple with powdered ginger is great, too! Get creative and try all kinds of flavors.

You can also marinate vegetables before dehydrating them. For example, I like marinating zucchini, bell peppers, carrots, mushrooms, or kale in tamari (wheat-free) and raw olive oil (or a mixture of raw olive oil and truffle oil). Sometimes I add seasoning to the mixture to spice it up or add some pizzazz.

Melons are fantastic when you dehydrate them. Dehydrate the seeds and eat them, too. Slice these fruits bigger, about an inch thick because of the high water content in them. They take longer, but it is worth the time.

Keep in mind that the size of the food you put in the dehydrator will be different than the size after it's done dehydrating. Fresh fruits and vegetables are made up mostly of water so don't be surprised when your tray "full" of fresh produce (before drying) comes out a fraction of the size (post drying), once the water is removed.

Zucchini Munchies

These are great to have around, particularly when you just want to munch on something. I love taking these to the movie theater. Then, I'm not tempted with popcorn.

> 2 medium zucchini
> ¼ cup raw olive oil
> 2 tablespoons fresh lemon juice
> 1 clove garlic, pressed
> ¼ teaspoon cumin
> ½ teaspoon Himalayan crystal salt
> ⅛ teaspoon cayenne
> ⅛ teaspoon paprika
> ¼ cup fresh parsley, minced

Slice the zucchini into thin rounds or lengthwise slices, using a mandoline or V-slicer (or knife) and place them in a bowl with the other ingredients, making sure to coat all the pieces. Wait 10–20 minutes. Transfer them to a dehydrator tray and lay them on it in a single layer without overlapping (be sure to shake off any excess oil first so they dehydrate better).

Dehydrate them at 140 degrees F for an hour. Lower the temperature to 105 degrees F and then continue dehydrating until you achieve your desired texture (about 10–24 hours or more, depending on the thickness).

Sun-Dried Tomatoes

These are super easy to make… even with no sun! Simply slice the tomatoes and dehydrate them until they're dry. That's it. The thinner you slice them, the faster they dry.

My mom and I love making sun-dried tomatoes using our dehydrators. Sometimes I sprinkle them with a little powdered garlic and fresh (or dried) basil before dehydrating.

Variations:

- After they're dehydrated, grind the tomatoes to a powder and use to season various dishes—yum!
- My mom loves to pour raw dressing over a handful of sun-dried tomatoes (just to lightly coat them). She lets them set like that in a bowl for 15–30 minutes as they soften. Then, she eats them like that or adds them to a salad, sandwich, or raw pasta dish.

Savory Garlic Zucchini Noodles

This is a really fun recipe that can be used in many ways.

- **¼ cup raw olive oil (more if needed)**
- **2–3 cloves garlic, pressed (and/or 1 inch ginger, peeled and grated)**
- **¾–1 teaspoon Himalayan crystal salt (or 1 tablespoon tamari, wheat-free)**
- **2 zucchini, spiralized**

Blend the oil, garlic and salt (or tamari) in a blender or shake thoroughly in a small jar. Spiralize the zucchini using a spiralizer. Then, toss the veggies with the marinade mixture in a bowl until well coated. Transfer the noodles to a dehydrator tray lined with a ParaFlexx sheet (shake off any excess oil first). Dehydrate at 140 degrees F for one hour. Lower the temperature to 105 degrees F and continue dehydrating until pliable or crisp, as desired. The less oil you use, the crispier they will be.

Serving suggestion:

- These are great served on top of raw soups, salads or as a garnish.

Zucchini with Garlic Sauce

Yield 2 servings

This is delicious as a side dish to any meal or it's a lovely snack any time of the day.

The Sauce

4–5 tablespoons raw olive oil

2 tablespoons fresh lemon juice

1 tablespoon tamari, wheat-free

1–2 cloves garlic, pressed

½ teaspoon onion powder

⅛ teaspoon black pepper

The Vegetables

2 cups zucchini, chopped

⅓ cup raw walnuts or raw pecans, chopped

Whisk together the sauce ingredients in a bowl and set aside. Put the zucchini in a shallow glass baking dish or bowl and pour the sauce over the zucchini and toss to mix. Place it in your dehydrator for 1–2 hours at 130–140 degrees F. Enjoy these warm from the dehydrator, topped with the chopped walnuts or pecans before serving.

Variation:

- Replace 1 cup of zucchini with 1 cup sliced mushrooms or chopped bell peppers.

Fun Leeks

Make a double or triple batch of this recipe so you'll have plenty on hand to garnish salads and soups.

1 ½ cups leeks, thinly sliced*

2 tablespoons raw olive oil

1 tablespoon tamari, wheat-free

1 teaspoon raw agave nectar

1 tablespoon fresh lemon juice

Rinse the sliced leeks (dirt likes to hide in leeks, so make sure you wash them really well). Whisk together the remaining ingredients in a bowl. Add in the sliced leeks and toss to thoroughly coat. Let these marinate for about 20 minutes (after ten minutes, stir to ensure even coverage).

Transfer them to a dehydrator tray (shaking off any excess oil over the bowl beforehand) and dehydrate at a temperature of 140 degrees F for one hour. Lower the temperature to 105 degrees F and continue dehydrating until crispy-ish, which is approximately 7–10 hours (or more).

* I use a handheld V-slicer (see KristensRaw.com/store).

Truffle Zucchini Flats

½ cup raw olive oil

2 teaspoons truffle oil

1 large clove garlic (or more!)

1 teaspoon Himalayan crystal salt

2 zucchini, thinly sliced lengthwise

Blend the olive oil, truffle oil, garlic and salt in a blender. Lay out the zucchini slices on dehydrator trays. Brush the zucchini slices (using a pastry brush) to just lightly coat them with the oil mixture on one side only.

Dehydrate at 140 degrees F for one hour. Lower the temperature to 105 degrees F and continue dehydrating until pliable or crisp, as desired. When you take them out of the dehydrator, you can blot them with paper towel to absorb excess oil, if desired.

Plant Leather

See photo at KristensRaw.com/photos.

Remember fruit roll-ups when you were growing up? Well, here is the healthy version, known as plant leather. Kids love it... and so do I! You can make "plant leather" snacks from many different fruits and vegetables. This is a tasty and chewy dried treat that is made by simply pureeing fruits and/or vegetables and dehydrating.

Here are some great ideas for making your own healthy version of the fruit roll-up. Have your kids help you (getting them involved makes them excited to eat it and show it off to their friends). One of the things you can do to make this extra special for kids is to cut the leather into shapes using scissors once the plant leather is dry and pliable.

Directions for Making the Best Plant Leather

For the following recipes, blend the ingredients listed in the recipe together (you can add a little water if needed to help facilitate the blending). If you don't have a blender with a plunger to help push the ingredients down, simply stop the blender every few seconds so you can scrape the sides and push the fruit and/or vegetables down into the blades.

If fresh herbs are used, I typically like to pulse them in after I have the main components already blended, so I can see the flecks of color of the briefly pulsed herbs.

Use approximately two cups of pureed fruit for every dehydrator tray and spread it evenly with an offset spatula (about ⅛–¼ inch thick) onto a dehydrator tray lined with a ParaFlexx sheet. Dehydrate for 1–2 hours at 140 degrees F.

Then, lower the temperature to 105 degrees F and continue dehydrating for another 7–12 hours (*or more, if needed*). Flip the Plant Leather over onto the mesh dehydrator sheet and peel off the ParaFlexx sheet. Continue dehydrating until dry, usually another 5–8 hours, or more.

Before storing, you can cut them into different shapes with scissors or you can roll them up in wax paper and store them in airtight glass mason jars in your refrigerator or freezer.

Things to Keep in Mind When Making Plant Leather

Use ripe produce and remove any stems or seeds (as needed). Cut the fruit into chunks and puree it. Add 2 teaspoons of lemon juice (optional) and 1–3 teaspoons (or more) of a sweetener if the fruit is tart (this is also optional).

The higher the sugar content in the leather, the longer the drying time. Sugar can make it quite sticky. Some fruits and vegetables result in more uniform Plant Leather and they dehydrate in one nice big piece. Some other combinations dry with cracks and crevices, but they all taste great!

You can also add variety to plant leathers with things such as sunflower seeds, ground flax seeds, sesame seeds, shredded unsweetened coconut, chia seeds, fresh herbs, etc. Just blend them right along with the fruit and vegetables or stir them in after. It's up to you!

Some people love to dehydrate their yogurt into leather. Next time you make coconut yogurt, puree some apple or pineapple (for example) into it and dehydrate it for a great treat.

Plant leather will generally take from 10–24 hours to dry the puree into leather.

A GREAT TIP: If you're dehydrating something that is really sticky and you can't get it off the dehydrator sheet, then putting the tray in the freezer can help. However, if you're using the ParaFlexx sheets from Excalibur, you shouldn't have any trouble with this.

Here are just a few recipes to get you started. You'll see how easy they are and the opportunities are endless with all of the mixing and matching you can do with fresh produce. So, be creative and have fun.

If your blender container isn't large enough to handle some of the recipes, simply blend the ingredients in batches and then transfer to a bowl where you can stir them together before dehydrating.

TROPICAL BLISS

1 mango, peeled and pitted
½ pineapple, peeled and chopped
1 Golden Delicious apple, cored and chopped
1 teaspoon fresh lime juice

Variation:

- After blending the fruit, stir in 2–4 tablespoons of shredded, unsweetened dried coconut.

CINNAMON APPLE AFTERNOON

3 apples, cored and chopped

2 bananas, peeled

½ teaspoon cinnamon

2 teaspoons fresh lemon juice

BLACKBERRY PEACH PARADE

3 peaches, pitted and chopped

1 cup blackberries

1 apple, cored and chopped

1 teaspoon fresh lime juice, optional

BANANA BLACKBERRY BLAST

2 cups blackberries

3 bananas, peeled and chopped

2 pinches nutmeg

1 teaspoon fresh lime juice, optional

STRAWBERRY COCONUT SENSATION

See photo at KristensRaw.com/photos.

2 cups strawberries

2 apples, cored and chopped

⅓ cup dried coconut, shredded and unsweetened

STRAWBERRY APPLE BASIL

2 cups strawberries

2 apples, cored and chopped

¼ cup fresh basil, chopped

PINEAPPLE GINGER PASSION

See photo at KristensRaw.com/photos.

½ pineapple, peeled and chopped

1 Golden Delicious apple, cored and chopped

1 ½ tablespoons fresh ginger, grated

Variation:

- For extra beautiful Pineapple Ginger Passion plant leather, pulse in 2–4 tablespoons of fresh chopped cilantro after pureeing the pineapple, apple, and ginger.

TOMATO MARINARA LEATHER

Don't throw away left over marinara sauce. Make delicious to-mato leather out of it. It's fabulous and fun. This also makes wonderful rustic-style chips for dipping into your favorite raw cheese or hummus. After making the leather, break (or tear) it into chips and enjoy.

VANILLA MINT STRAWBERRY

3 cups strawberries, chopped

2 pears, cored and chopped

½ teaspoon vanilla extract

¼ cup fresh mint, chopped

STRAWBERRY BANANA DANCE

2 cups strawberries, chopped

2 bananas, peeled

2 teaspoons fresh lime juice

IT'S POLISH TIME

See photo at KristensRaw.com/photos.

1 large beet, trimmed and chopped

2 apples, cored and chopped

1 teaspoon dry mustard, more to taste

3 tablespoons fresh dill

Serving suggestion:

- Cut squares and serve topped with raw, unpasteurized sauerkraut.

HOLIDAY SEASON LEATHER

1 pear, cored and chopped

1 apple, cored and chopped

2 carrots, chopped

2 teaspoons raw agave nectar (or more)

1 teaspoon pumpkin pie spice

BANANA NUT FUSION

See photo at KristensRaw.com/photos.

2 bananas, peeled and chopped

1 Golden Delicious apple, cored and chopped

¼ cup nuts, finely chopped

a little water, as needed

3
· · ·

Nuts & Seeds

So many people spend their health gaining wealth, and then have to spend their wealth to regain their health.

A. J. REB MATERI

Basic instructions for soaking and dehydrating plain nuts and seeds can be found in Appendix A. Once you are familiar with these quick basics, there are many ways to add extra pizzazz to your dehydrated nuts and seeds!

Simply Sweet Pumpkin Seeds

Yield approximately 4–5 servings

I love sprinkling these on top of my salads to give it a little crunch and a touch of sweetness. Pumpkin seeds are an excellent source of zinc, magnesium, phosphorus, iron, copper, manganese, and vitamin K.

1 cup raw pumpkin seeds

2 tablespoons raw agave nectar

½ teaspoon cinnamon

½ teaspoon vanilla extract

⅛ teaspoon Himalayan crystal salt

Place the pumpkin seeds in a bowl with enough water to cover by about an inch. Let them soak on your countertop for 6–8 hours. Drain off the water and give them a quick rinse.

Place the soaked seeds in a bowl and stir in the remaining ingredients. Spread the mixture onto a dehydrator tray lined with a ParaFlexx sheet and dehydrate at 140 degrees F for about an hour. Reduce the temperature to 105 degrees F and dehydrate another 16–24 hours or until they are dry.

Candied Maple Nuts

Yield 3 cups

These are so delicious. They make a great gift, too. I like to buy cute little jars and fill them with these, and give them out during the holidays (or for special occasions like birthdays, retirement, etc).

2 cups raw nuts

¼ cup raw agave nectar

1 ½ teaspoons cinnamon

1 teaspoon maple extract

¼ teaspoon Himalayan crystal salt

Place the nuts in a bowl with enough water to cover by about an inch. Let them soak on your countertop for 6–8 hours. Drain off the water and give them a quick rinse.

Combine the agave, cinnamon, maple extract and salt in a small bowl and stir. Place the soaked nuts in a separate bowl and stir in the agave mixture, making sure the nuts are evenly coated.

Spread out on a dehydrator tray (fitted with a ParaFlexx sheet — make sure you use all the syrup and drizzle any remaining in the bowl on top of the nuts). Dehydrate at 140 degrees F for about an hour. Reduce the temperature to 105 degrees F and dehydrate another 18–24 hours or until they are dry.

Sticky Ginger Orange Cashews

Yield approximately 2 cups

Sticky, delicious, and nutritious — that is the perfect description for these delectable nuts.

½ cup + 1 tablespoon fresh orange juice

¼ cup water

1 ¼ cups raw cashews

2 tablespoons raw agave nectar

1 tablespoon fresh ginger, grated and gently packed

1 tablespoon fresh orange zest, grated

pinch Himalayan crystal salt

Place the cashews in a bowl with ½ cup of the orange juice and water (reserve the 1 tablespoon of orange juice for use later). Let the cashews soak like this on your countertop for 3-4 hours. Drain off the juice and water (do not rinse). Place the soaked cashews in a medium bowl, and stir in the agave, ginger, orange zest, 1 tablespoon of orange juice, and salt. Stir until the cashews are coated.

Spread the cashews out on a dehydrator tray fitted with a ParaFlexx sheet (make sure you use all of the syrup mixture and drizzle any remaining in the bowl on top of the cashews). Dehydrate at 140 degrees F for about an hour. Reduce the temperature to 105 degrees F and dehydrate another 24–36 hours or until they're dry.

Amazing Munchies

These are perfect for travel, hiking, going to the movies (so you stay away from the popcorn!), topping your salads or stirring into raw vegan soups.

> **2 cups raw pumpkin seeds or raw sunflower seeds (or a mixture)**
>
> **3 tablespoons tamari, wheat-free**
>
> **2 tablespoons fresh lime juice**
>
> **1 teaspoon Chili powder**
>
> **½ teaspoon onion powder**
>
> **½ teaspoon garlic powder**

Place the seeds in a bowl with enough water to cover by about an inch. Let them soak on your countertop for 6–8 hours. Drain off the water and give them a quick rinse.

Transfer them to a bowl and add the remaining ingredients. Stir to incorporate well. Spread the seed mixture on a dehydrator tray.

Dehydrate at 140 degrees F for one hour. Lower the temperature to 105 degrees F and dehydrate until dry (16–24 hours, or more).

Chewy Bolder Boulder Granola

See photo at KristensRaw.com/photos.

Yield approximately 6 cups of batter

When you want something hearty, satiating and sweet, this is the answer. It's so easy and fun to make; trust me!

½ cup raw pecans

½ cup raw walnuts

½ cup raw pumpkin seeds

½ cup raw sesame seeds

¼ cup raw sunflower seeds

1 ¼ cups water

1 ½ cups Medjool dates, pitted and packed (approximately 25 dates)

1 ½ teaspoons cinnamon

pinch Himalayan crystal salt

pinch nutmeg

½ cup raisins

½ cup dried cranberries

½ cup dried coconut, shredded and unsweetened

½ cup hemp seeds

3 tablespoons raw cacao nibs

Place the pecans, walnuts, pumpkin seeds, sesame seeds, and sunflower seeds in a bowl (or use a couple of bowls if needed) with enough water to cover by about an inch. Let them soak on your countertop for 6–8 hours. Drain off the water and give them a quick rinse.

Place the water in your blender. Loosely separate the dates and add them along with the cinnamon, salt, and nutmeg to the blender. Blend until smooth. In a large bowl, combine the remaining ingredients, including the soaked nuts/seeds, and toss to mix. Add the date mixture to the bowl and stir together with a rubber spatula until the date mixture is evenly distributed over the nut/seed mixture (or, for sticky fun, use your hands!) *See photos, below.*

Place 4 cups of the batter on a dehydrator tray fitted with a ParaFlexx, non-stick sheet. Spread it evenly using an offset spatula to approximately ¼ inch thickness. Repeat until all of the batter is used. *If you're going to make these as granola "bars", then make them ½ inch thick and go ahead and score them into bars now.*

Dehydrate Chewy Bolder Boulder Granola at 130–140 degrees F for about one hour. Lower the temperature to 105 degrees F and continue dehydrating for about 8–10 hours. Flip the granola over onto a regular mesh dehydrator tray and peel off the ParaFlexx sheet. Continue dehydrating another 16–24 hours, or until dry. If making the granola in the form of bars, you'll probably want to continue dehydrating them longer since they are thicker.

Break the granola apart into desired size chunks and enjoy it plain or with fresh raw nut or seed milk.

Variations:

- Add more dates to make a sweeter granola.
- Add 1 teaspoon vanilla extract or add a minced whole vanilla bean to the date mixture before blending.
- Add fresh grated ginger for a delicious and extra nutritious treat.

STEP 1. Place the blended ingredients with the other ingredients in a large bowl.

STEP 2. Stir together with a rubber spatula until the mixture is evenly distributed over the nuts/seeds.

STEP 3. Place the mixture onto a dehydrator tray lined with a ParaFlexx sheet.

STEP 4. Spread evenly using an offset spatula to approximately ¼-inch thickness.

Sunny Italian Patties

Yield approximately 3 ½ cups

1 cup raw sunflower seeds or raw pumpkin seeds,

½ cup raw walnuts

¾ cup sun-dried tomatoes

1 ½ tablespoons sun-dried tomato powder*

1 tablespoon fresh lemon juice

1 tablespoon tamari, wheat-free

1 ½ teaspoons fennel seed, ground

2 cloves garlic, pressed

⅛ teaspoon black pepper

dash cayenne pepper

2 tablespoons red onion, minced

¼ cup fresh basil, chopped or 1 ½ tablespoons dried

1 tablespoon fresh rosemary, minced or 1 teaspoon dried

2 teaspoons fresh oregano, chopped or ½ teaspoon dried

Place the sunflower seeds (or pumpkin seeds) and walnuts in a bowl with enough water to cover by about an inch. Let them soak on your countertop for 6–8 hours. Drain off the water and give them a quick rinse.

Place the sun-dried tomatoes in a bowl with enough water just to cover them. Let them soak on your countertop for about an hour. Drain off the soak water and reserve it for use later in the recipe. Chop the sun-dried tomatoes.

Place all of the ingredients except the onion, basil, rosemary, and oregano in a food processor, fitted with the "S" blade. Process until you get a pate consistency, adding soak water from the sun-dried tomatoes, if necessary. Add the onion, basil, rosemary and oregano and pulse until mixed.

Form into ¼-cup patties and place them into your dehydrator at 140 degrees F for one hour. Lower the temperature to 105 degrees F and continue dehydrating for another 4–8 hours. At this point they're perfect for eating (yum!) or you can freeze them and gobble them up later.

Variations:

- Instead of making patties, you can roll these into balls for "meat" balls and enjoy with Raw vegan zucchini pasta.
- Add 2–4 tablespoons raisins or currants when processing the ingredients (seeds, nuts, etc.).

* To make sun-dried tomato powder, dehydrate fresh tomatoes. Then, grind your dehydrated tomatoes in a dry blender, food processor or coffee grinder. Stored in a glass mason jar, the powder will keep for months in the refrigerator.

4
...

Pancakes, Crackers, Breads & Wraps

A man's health can be judged by which he takes two at a time—pills or stairs.

JOAN WELSH

This chapter includes some of my favorite recipes... pancakes anyone?! Yum! My husband loves when I have a stash of those in the refrigerator. He snacks on them cold, right from the fridge.

Kristen Suzanne's Famous Pancakes

See photo on cover and at KristensRaw.com/photos.

Yield 2 ¾ cups batter or 10–13 pancakes

These are simply amazing, and much healthier than using flour. Kids love them! And after breakfast, they make great snacks.

> ⅓ cup raw macadamia nuts, unsoaked
>
> 1 cup raw Brazil nuts, unsoaked
>
> ¾ cup flax meal
>
> 2 bananas, peeled
>
> 1 apple, cored and chopped
>
> ½ cup + 1 tablespoon water
>
> ½ teaspoon cinnamon
>
> ½ teaspoon vanilla extract
>
> pinch nutmeg
>
> pinch Himalayan crystal salt

Using a food processor, fitted with the "S" blade, grind the macadamia nuts and Brazil nuts to a fine texture. Add the flax meal to the food processor with the ground nuts and pulse a few times to incorporate.

In your blender, puree the remaining ingredients. Add the nut/flax mixture to the blender and blend to mix. If you don't have a high-powered blender you might have to do this in two batches. Using ¼ cup measuring cup and an offset spatula, spread the batter into little pancakes (⅛–¼ inch thick) on a dehydrator tray, fitted with a ParaFlexx sheet.

Dehydrate your pancakes at 140 degrees F for one hour. Lower the temperature to 105 degrees F and continue dehydrating another 3–4 hours. Flip the pancakes onto the mesh dehydrator sheet and peel off the ParaFlexx sheet. Continue dehydrating 4–6 hours (or until your desired texture is achieved).

Drizzle with Sweet Maple Sauce, Raw Maple Syrup, or Easy Fruit Syrup (see recipes, below).

Sweet Maple Sauce

See photo on cover and at KristensRaw.com/photos.

Yield 1 ¾ cups

Dates are nature's candy and they make this sauce sweetly nutritious.

- 1 ¼ cups water
- 11 soft dates, pitted
- 1 tablespoon maple extract

Blend all of the ingredients until smooth. Serve with Kristen Suzanne's Famous Pancakes or over any chopped fruit for a delicious meal—especially bananas!

Raw Maple Syrup

Yield ½ cup

Traditional maple syrup is not raw. If you're looking for a quick and easy raw version of maple syrup that "looks like syrup" instead of a sauce, this is the answer.

½ cup raw dark agave nectar*
2 teaspoons maple extract (or more to taste)

Stir the ingredients together in a bowl. Serve with Kristen Suzanne's Famous Pancakes or over any chopped fruit for a fun meal or dessert.

* Note: If possible, get a brand that claims to be both raw and not heated above 118 degrees F. The brand I use for raw dark agave nectar is *Wholesome Sweeteners' Organic Raw Blue Agave.*

Easy Fruit Syrup

Yield 1–1 ½ cups

This easy recipe is great with any fruit you choose. My favorites are blueberries, raspberries, strawberries, cherries… aww, who am I kidding? It's terrific with any fruit.

1 16oz. bag of any organic frozen fruit, thawed

¼ cup raw agave nectar

Blend the ingredients until smooth. Serve with Kristen Suzanne's Famous Pancakes or over any chopped fruit for a super delicious, high-energy meal.

Savory Cranberry Bread

Yield approximately 2 dehydrator trays of bread

This bread is beautiful because it is full of confetti-like colors. It's perfect for the holidays or any celebration!

- 1 pound onions, peeled and chopped (get a mix of red and white)
- 1 zucchini, chopped
- 1 cup cherry or grape tomatoes
- ¼ cup + 2 tablespoons dried cranberries
- ⅓ cup ground flax seeds
- ⅔ cup ground raw pumpkin seeds or raw sunflower seeds
- 3 tablespoons raw agave nectar
- ¼ cup tamari, wheat-free
- ¼ cup fresh basil, chopped

Process the onions, zucchini, tomatoes, and dried cranberries in a food processor, fitted with the "S" blade, into small pieces, but don't let it get to a mush. Set aside in a large bowl. Add the remaining ingredients and mix well by hand. Use 2–3 cups of batter and spread it onto each ParaFlexx-covered dehydrator tray.

Dehydrate for one hour at 140 degrees F. Lower the temperature for the remainder of the dehydrating time to 105 degrees F. Dehydrate for another 6–8 hours. Flip the bread over onto a mesh dehydrator sheet, remove the ParaFlexx sheet and dehydrate another 6–10 hours until the desired dryness is achieved. Cut into desired shape and size.

Garlic Oregano Crackers

Yield 1 dehydrator tray

These crackers are easy and delightful.

½ cup flax seeds

½ cup chia seeds

¼ cup raw olive oil

¾ cup water, more if needed

1 medium tomato

2 tablespoons fresh oregano leaves, chopped

1 tablespoon Italian seasoning

2–3 cloves garlic

2 tablespoons fresh lime juice

2 tablespoons raw agave nectar

½ teaspoon Himalayan crystal salt

½ teaspoon onion powder

pinch black pepper

Grind the flax and chia seeds into a powder using either a coffee grinder or a dry blender. Then, place the ground flax and chia seeds into a large bowl and set aside.

Blend the remaining ingredients and add the blended mixture to the bowl with the dry seed mixture. Mix well by hand (adding more water if needed). Spread the batter onto a ParaFlexx-covered dehydrator tray. Score them to the desired size. Dehydrate for one hour at 140 degrees F.

Lower the temperature for the remainder of the dehydrating time to 105 degrees F. Dehydrate for another 6–8 hours. Flip them over onto the mesh dehydrator sheet, remove the ParaFlexx sheet and dehydrate another 6–10 hours until desired dryness is achieved.

Serving suggestions:

- I love using these for pizza crusts and as a delicious cracker or bread for raw cheese or hummus.

Banana Biscuits

Yield 6–8 biscuits

Warning: if you sample these while they're dehydrating, you might end up eating them all before they're done "cooking."

> **1 cup fresh nut pulp, packed***
> **2 bananas, peeled**
> **3–5 tablespoons water**

Place the nut pulp and bananas in a food processor, fitted with the "S" blade and begin processing until thoroughly mixed. Add the water, as needed.

Spread the mixture on to a dehydrator tray, fitted with a ParaFlexx sheet until it is about ½ inch thick. Dehydrate at 135 degrees F for 45 minutes. Take them out of the dehydrator and score into desired shape and size. Reduce the temperature to 105 degrees F and continue dehydrating 8–10 hours. Flip the biscuits onto a mesh tray (without ParaFlexx) and peel off the ParaFlexx sheet currently being used. Dehydrate another 8–10 hours, or until dry.

* Nut pulp is left over after making nut milk and straining it in a nut milk bag. The moist pulp in the bag is the nut pulp.

Strawberry Sweet Bread

See photo at KristensRaw.com/photos.

Yield 6–9 pieces

This recipe is loaded with essential fatty acids, antioxidants, fiber, vitamins, and minerals. When it's time to send your kids to school, give them a nutritious lunch by including this. Oh... and.... my husband loves this snack, too. I mean he really LOVES it! It's great for the whole family.

> 1 cup raw cashews
>
> 1 cup Twister Sprouted Omega Blend*
>
> ¾ cup fresh orange juice
>
> 2 cups strawberries, chopped
>
> 2 cups zucchini, chopped
>
> 2 teaspoons ginger powder
>
> 1 ¼ teaspoons vanilla extract
>
> 1 teaspoon orange peel powder** or orange zest
>
> ½ teaspoon Himalayan crystal salt
>
> ¼ teaspoon stevia powder (optional)

Grind the cashews to a fine grind using a blender or food processor (fitted with the "S" blade). Transfer to a large bowl. Add the Twister Blend to the bowl and stir to mix the ingredients. Blend the remaining ingredients together using a blender. Transfer the blended mixture to the bowl with the cashew/Twister ingredients, and stir thoroughly to mix. Loosely cover the bowl with a piece of paper towel (or cloth towel), and let it sit on your counter for 2 hours.

Spread all of the bread dough on a dehydrator tray lined with a non-stick ParaFlexx sheet. It should be about 10" x 10" with a height (or thickness) of about ½". Dehydrate at 135 degrees F for one hour. Reduce the temperature to 105–110 degrees F and continue dehydrating another 8–10 hours.

Flip the bread onto a tray that is not lined with a ParaFlexx sheet. Peel off the current sheet of ParaFlexx being used. Continue dehydrating 10–12 hours. Cut the bread into desired size pieces and continue dehydrating another 1–4 hours, or more, depending on desired dryness. The goal is not to dry the bread completely if you want it like a soft bread.

* If you don't have Navitas Naturals' *Twister Sprouted Omega Blend*, you can use a mixture of ground flax seeds and ground chia seeds.

** See Appendix B: Resources.

Carrot Herb Crackers

Yield 20 crackers

These are easy and fabulous. No soaking or "pre" steps required. Make a few batches and have them on hand to snack on all the time.

- ½ cup flax seeds
- ½ cup chia seeds
- ¼ cup coconut oil
- ¾ cup water, more, if needed*
- 1 cup carrots, chopped
- ⅓ cup fresh basil, packed
- 1 teaspoon dried rosemary
- 2 cloves garlic
- Juice from ½ lemon
- ½ teaspoon Himalayan crystal salt

Use your blender or coffee grinder to grind the flax and chia seeds into a fine grind. Transfer them to a large bowl. Blend the remaining ingredients until smooth. Pour the blended mixture into the bowl with the flax and chia meal and stir by hand quickly to mix (adding a little more water if needed).

Spread the batter (using an offset spatula and/or your hands) onto a dehydrator tray lined with a ParaFlexx sheet—I leave mine with a touch of thickness, but you can spread as thick or thin, as you like.

Score them to the desired size (I score about 20 medium sized crackers). Dehydrate at 140 degrees F for one hour. Flip the crackers onto another dehydrator tray without ParaFlexx and peel off the ParaFlexx. At this point you might be able to break them apart by the scored lines you made. Continue dehydrating at 105 degrees F until dry (6–10 hours or more).

Variations and serving suggestions:

- Add some kick with cayenne pepper and Mexican seasoning.
- Dip these into raw soups, purees, or pates.
- Spread into rounds before dehydrating and make delicious pizza crusts.

---

* I prefer using ¾ cup water, which makes the batter thick, so you have to work with it quickly. However, you can use more water, adding a little as you go, until you get a consistency you can easily spread out.

Chocolate Hemp Bars

Yield 1–2 dehydrator trays full (depending on thickness desired)

⅔ cup flax seeds

2 cups water, more if necessary

1 ½ cups hemp protein powder

¾ cup raw chocolate powder

1 apple, cored and chopped

1 banana, peeled

¼ cup raw agave nectar

1 teaspoon almond extract

½ teaspoon cinnamon

⅛ teaspoon Himalayan crystal salt

Grind the flax seeds into a fine grind, using either a dry blender or a coffee grinder, and set aside. Blend all of the remaining ingredients together in a blender or food processor. Pour the mixture into a large bowl and stir in the ground flax seeds (add more water if needed). Spread the mixture onto a dehydrator tray lined with a ParaFlexx sheet. If you're looking for a thicker, chewier bar, make it ¾ to 1-inch thick. Score into the desired shape.

Dehydrate at 140 degrees F for one to two hours. Lower the temperature to 105 degrees F and continue dehydrating another 6–10 hours. Flip the bars onto the mesh dehydrator sheet, remove the ParaFlexx sheet, and continue dehydrating another 6–8 hours or longer until you get the desired dryness in your bars.

Garlic Basil Chia Crackers

Yield 20 crackers

1 cup chia seeds

¼ cup raw olive oil

¾ to 1 cup water (more, if needed)

¼ cup fresh basil, packed

1 ½ teaspoons dried basil

3 cloves garlic

Juice from ½ lemon

½ teaspoon Himalayan crystal salt

Use your blender or coffee grinder to grind the chia seeds into a meal. Transfer the chia meal to a large bowl. Blend the remaining ingredients until smooth. Pour the blended mixture into the bowl with the chia meal and stir by hand quickly to mix.

Immediately spread the batter (using an offset spatula and/or your hands) onto a dehydrator tray lined with ParaFlexx. Score them to the desired size (I score about 20 medium sized crackers).

Dehydrate at 135 degrees F for about 45-minutes. Flip the crackers onto another dehydrator tray without a ParaFlexx sheet and peel off the ParaFlexx. At this point you might be able to break them apart by the scored lines you made. Continue dehydrating at 105 degrees F until dry (6–10 hours or more).

Coconut Ginger Wraps

Yield approximately 4 medium tortilla wraps

1 cup flax meal

4 young Thai coconuts (yield about 2 cups coconut meat)

1 ½ cups young Thai coconut water, more if necessary

1 teaspoon ginger powder

dash Himalayan crystal salt

Set your flax meal aside in a bowl. Blend the remaining ingredients in a blender until smooth. Stir the blended coconut mixture into the flax meal. If the batter is too thick, add a little more water so you have a nice consistency that spreads well. Spread onto a dehydrator tray lined with a ParaFlexx sheet, in the desired size of your wraps.

Dehydrate at 140 degrees F for about 30 minutes. Lower the temperature to 105 degrees F and dehydrate another few hours. Gently lift them up to see if they're ready to flip. If they are ready, then flip them onto the mesh dehydrator sheets and remove the ParaFlexx sheet. Dehydrate another few hours, until they're pliable, but not crispy dry or they won't wrap around your food.

If you dehydrate them too far, get a spray bottle and mist them lightly with water until they become more pliable for you.

Enjoy wrapped around some delicious chopped fruit, vegetables, and/or sprouts.

Fun Corn Chips

Yield approximately 2 trays of corn chips

4 cups fresh corn cut from the cob, or frozen corn (thawed)

½ cup water

1 ½ teaspoons Himalayan crystal salt

1 ½ teaspoons cumin

2 teaspoons chili or Mexican seasoning

½ cup flax meal

1 tablespoon poppy seeds, optional

Blend the corn, water and salt in a blender on high speed until smooth. Add the cumin and chili seasoning and blend briefly. Add the ground flax seeds and poppy seeds, and blend briefly on low speed until mixed together.

Spread the batter between two dehydrator trays lined with ParaFlexx sheets, using an offset spatula (the thinner the layer of batter, the crispier they will be). Score the batter into the size of Fun Corn Chips you desire.

Dehydrate at 140 degrees F for 1–2 hours. Reduce the temperature to 105 degrees F and continue dehydrating another 6–8 hours. Remove the ParaFlexx sheet by flipping the sheet over onto a mesh dehydrator tray. Gently peel off the ParaFlexx sheet. Continue dehydrating at 105 degrees F for 8–10 hours until they have a chewy but crispy texture.

5
· · ·

Special Dehydrated Ingredients

Health is the greatest possession. Contentment is the greatest treasure. Confidence is the greatest friend. Non-being is the greatest joy.

LAO TZU

This chapter includes great, fun, and unique ways to use your dehydrator with various ingredients.

Almond Pulp

Using Almond Pulp as Flour for Raw Cakes, Brownies, and Cookies

You may see raw food recipes calling for "almond pulp," which is easy to make. After making Almond Nut Milk (see recipe, below) and straining it through a nut milk bag, there is a nice, soft pulp inside the bag.

Turn the bag inside out and flatten the pulp on a ParaFlexx-covered tray with a spatula. Dehydrate at 140 degrees F for one hour, then lower the temperature to 105 degrees F and continue dehydrating until the pulp is dry (up to 24 hours).

Break the pulp into chunks and freeze until needed. Before using the almond pulp, grind it into flour in your blender or food processor.

Almond Nut Milk

Yield 4–5 cups

If you desire sweeter milk, add 1–2 pitted dates or 1–2 table-spoons of raw agave nectar.

1 ½ cups raw almonds

3 ¼ cups water, more if desired

pinch Himalayan crystal salt, optional

Place the almonds in a bowl with enough water to cover by about an inch. Let them soak on your countertop for 8–10 hours. Drain off the water and give them a quick rinse.

Blend the ingredients until smooth and creamy. For an extra creamy texture, strain the milk through a nut milk bag and reserve the almond pulp for dehydrating (above).

Raw Cheese Sprinkle

Yield 2 cups

1 ½ cups pine nuts

2 cloves garlic

⅛ teaspoon cayenne

1 tablespoon tamari, wheat-free

2 tablespoons lemon juice

¼ teaspoon probiotic powder (about 2 capsules worth)

water, for mixing

Place the pine nuts in a bowl with enough water to cover by about an inch. Let them soak on your countertop for 1–2 hours. Drain off the water and give them a quick rinse. Blend all of the ingredients together, using water as needed to get the mixture going. Spread the cheese mixture thinly onto a dehydrator tray lined with a ParaFlexx sheet and let it sit out on your countertop for 2–3 hours. (Use more than one tray if needed.)

Dehydrate the mixture at 130 degrees F for 20–40 minutes. Lower the temperature to 105 degrees F and continue dehydrating another 6–8 hours or until you can flip the cheese over onto the mesh dehydrator sheet and remove the ParaFlexx sheet. Continue dehydrating another 6–10 hours, or until dry.

At this point, you should be able to crush the cheese into a crumble by hand.

Dried Herbs

In my opinion, it doesn't get much better than this when it comes to flavor. It's great to make your own freshly dried herbs. Talk about healthy and full of flavor! All you have to do is wash your fresh herbs and dehydrate them until thoroughly dry. It's helpful to place a mesh tray screen on top of the herbs as they dry, so that when they get close to completely dry (and they're super light in weight) they won't fly around the inside of the dehydrator as the air blows around.

Store the whole dried leaves in glass mason jars and take them out as needed. When you're ready to use them, crush them with your fingers for the amount you need. It's best to store dehydrated herbs in the whole leaf form. This maintains the fullest flavor of the herbs.

Garlic

Garlic can be dehydrated whole or sliced. My favorite way is to peel and slice the garlic, then dehydrate it for 10–16 hours (or more) until it's completely dehydrated. You can store it, as is, in a glass mason jar or grind it to a powder in a blender or coffee grinder before using.

Horseradish

Horseradish is great dehydrated and added to recipes like raw vegan salad dressings, cheese, dips, and soups. It adds a wonderful warming component that you experience when eating it. I love horseradish.

All you have to do is wash the fresh horseradish root, peel or scrape it and then grate it. Dehydrate 10–18 hours (or more) until it's completely dehydrated.

Parsley or Cilantro

I love dehydrating parsley and cilantro, so I always have it on hand to sprinkle on top of soups, salads, or throw into my smoothies. Simply wash the parsley or cilantro thoroughly, separate the clusters, cut off the long stems and dehydrate for 7–10 hours (or more) until completely dehydrated.

Celery as a Salty Flavoring

This is considered the mega healthy alternative for adding a salty flavoring to your food, while keeping the sodium content low. This is the kind of salt you'll find some Natural Hygienists using.

It's easy to make. Take your celery stalks and pull off some strings, if possible. Chop the celery and dehydrate it until thoroughly dry. Grind it to a powder using your coffee grinder or blender. When you want a little added salt flavor in your recipes while still keeping it mega-healthy, just use some of this.

COLORING FOODS

Organic Edible Flowers Make Beautiful Colors

Organic edible flowers come in all kinds of beautiful colors and they're not just for salads and garnish anymore. I love using them in other recipes too for added nutrition as well as flare!

They give you the opportunity to add beautiful colors to ordinary light-colored dishes.

Did you know that organic edible flowers are rich in nectar and pollen? Studies have shown pollen to be full of minerals and vitamins. Roses, especially rose hips, are very high in vitamin C. Dandelion blossoms (and yellow flowers, in general) have plenty of vitamin A, while the leaves are loaded with iron, calcium, phosphorous and vitamins A and C. Marigolds and Nasturtium are rich in vitamin C.

Here's how to use them. Buy organic edible flowers and dehydrate them by placing them on your mesh dehydrator tray, and like the process for dehydrating fresh herbs, place another mesh sheet on top. This prevents them from flying all over the dehydrator once most of the water is removed and they're super light in weight. Divide them by color (purples and blues, pinks and reds, yellows and oranges). Pull off any green parts so you primarily have the petals. Then, grind them to a powder (or extra fine grind) with a coffee grinder. Now, you can use these as a delicious and nutritious food coloring. I use them in foods like raw cheese, raw frostings and sweet raw glazes to add extra fun and diversity in my presentation. See the following recipe to get you started.

Alternatively, after dehydrating the flowers, you can use them as decoration because now you have beautiful potpourri.

Lavender Sweet Glaze

Yield 1 cup

¾ cup young Thai coconut meat

½ cup young Thai coconut water

2 tablespoons raw agave nectar

1 tablespoon (or more) of dried purple organic edible
flowers, ground

Blend the coconut meat, coconut water and agave until very smooth. Add the dried flowers and blend well.

Serving suggestions:

- Use this sweet glaze on top of raw cakes and ice creams.
- Serve as a sweet dip for fresh fruit and vegetables.

Variations:

- To intensify the color, add another 1–2 teaspoons of dried edible flowers.
- To use on savory dishes, make the recipe without the agave so you're just getting a mild coconut flavor.

Zucchini Colors, Too!

You can also do the same thing with zucchini skin. Peel off the green skin and dehydrate it. Then, grind it to a powder and you have some nutritious green coloring for your next batch of cheese or frosting.

Beet Is Beautiful for Coloring Your Food

Beets make a great all natural food coloring. Dehydrate very thin slices of fresh beet until thoroughly dry. Then, grind the dried beets to a powder or fine grind. When you need a little pink or red color for something, add a teaspoon or more to whatever you're making—dressings, cheeses, desserts, etc. Or, try the recipes below showcasing how beets can add color.

Red Holiday Coconut

Here is a quick and easy way to add color to your coconut. This is beautiful sprinkled on desserts, salads, or entrees.

¼ cup dried coconut, shredded and unsweetened

2 tablespoons fresh beet juice

Stir the coconut and beet juice together in a bowl. Spread the mixture onto a dehydrator tray lined with a ParaFlexx sheet. Dehydrate until dry (6–12 hours).

Hot Pink Candy Crumble

Yield approximately 2 cups

This sweet little dish is so fun, pretty and easy to make. What a great way to have cauliflower (it never tasted so great!).

> 3 tablespoons fresh orange juice
>
> 1 tablespoon fresh lemon juice
>
> 3 tablespoons raw agave nectar
>
> 2 pinches of stevia powder, optional
>
> ¼–⅓ cup fresh beet juice*
>
> 1 head cauliflower florets, rough chopped
>
> ½ cup dried coconut, shredded and unsweetened

Place the orange juice, lemon juice, agave, stevia, and beet juice in a large bowl. Process the cauliflower in a food processor, fitted with the "S" blade, until you get the consistency of rice.

Transfer the cauliflower to the bowl with the beet juice mixture. Add the coconut and stir everything together until it's thoroughly mixed. Spread the mixture onto a dehydrator tray lined with a ParaFlexx sheet. Dehydrate at 135 degrees F for one hour. Lower the temperature to 105 degrees F and continue drying for 8–12 hours (or overnight).

* To make a lighter pink color, start with 2 tablespoons of beet juice and go from there.

Appendix A
•••••••••••
Raw Basics

This "Raw Basics" appendix is a brief introduction to Raw for those who are new to the subject. It is the same in all of my recipe books.

WHY RAW?

Living the Raw vegan lifestyle has made me a more effective person... in everything I do. I get to experience pure, sustainable all-day-long energy. My body is in perfect shape and I gain strength and endurance in my exercise routine with each passing day. My relationships are the best they've ever been, because I'm happy and I love myself and my life. My headaches have ceased to exist, and my skin glows with the radiance of brand new life, which is exactly how I feel. Raw vegan is the best thing that has ever happened to me.

Whatever your passion is in life (family, business, exercise, meditation, hobbies, etc.), eating Raw vegan will take it to unbelievable new heights. Raw vegan food offers you the most amazing benefits—physically, mentally, and spiritually. It is *the* ideal choice for your food consumption if you want to become the healthiest and best "you" possible. Raw vegan food is for people who want to live longer while feeling younger. It's for people who want to feel vibrant and alive, and want to enjoy life like never before. All I ever have to say to someone is, "Just try it for yourself." It will change your life. From simple to gourmet, there's always something for everyone, and it's delicious. Come into the world of Raw with me, and experience for yourself the most amazing health *ever*.

Are you ready for your new lease on life? The time is now. Let's get started!

SOME GREAT THINGS TO KNOW BEFORE DIVING INTO THESE RECIPES

Organic Food

According to the Organic Trade Association, "Organic agricultural production benefits the environment by using earth-friendly agricultural methods and practices." Here are some facts that show why organic farming is "the way to grow."

Choosing organically grown foods is one of the most important choices we can make. According to Environmental Working Group, "The growing consensus among scientists is that small doses of some pesticides and other chemicals can cause lasting damage to human health, especially during fetal development and early childhood."

I use organic produce and products for pretty much everything when it comes to my food. There are very few exceptions, and that would be if the recipe called for something I just can't get organic such as jicama, certain seasonings, or any random ingredient that my local health food store is not able to procure from an organic grower for whatever reason.

If you think organic foods are too expensive, then start in baby steps and buy a few things at a time. Realize that you're probably going to spend less money in the long run on health problems as your health improves, and going organic is one way to facilitate that.

The more people who choose organic, the lower the prices will be in the long run. Until then, if people complain about the prices of organic produce, all I can say is, "Your health is worth it!" Personally, I'm willing to spend more on it and sacrifice other things in my life if necessary. I don't need the coolest car on the block, I want the healthiest food going into my body. I like what Alice Waters says, "Why wouldn't you want to spend most of your money on food? Food is nourishment and good health. It is the most important thing in life, really."

Vote with your dollar! Here is something I do to help further this cause and you can, too. When I eat at a restaurant I always write on the bill, "I would eat here more if you served organic food." Can you imagine what would happen if we all did this?

Bottom Line: It is essential to use organic ingredients for many reasons:

1. The health benefits—superior nutrition, reduced intake of chemicals and heavy metals and decreased exposure to carcinogens. Organic food has been shown to have up to 300% more nutrition than conventionally grown, non-organic produce. And, a very important note for pregnant women: pesticides could cross the placenta and get to the growing life inside of you. Make organics an extra priority if you are pregnant.

2. To have the very best tasting food ever—use organic ingredients! I've had people tell me in my raw food demonstration classes that they never knew vegetables tasted so good—and one of the main reasons is because I only use organic.

3. Greater variety of heirloom fruits and vegetables is the result of growing organic produce.

4. Cleaner rivers and waterways for our earth and its inhabitants, along with minimized topsoil erosion. Overall, organic farming builds up the soil better, reduces carbon dioxide from the air, and has many environmental benefits.

Going Organic on a Budget

Going organic on a budget is not impossible. Here are things to keep in mind that will help you afford it:

1. Buy in bulk. Ask the store you frequent if they'll give you a deal for buying certain foods by the case. (Just make sure it's a case of something that you can go through in a timely fashion so it doesn't go to waste). Consider this for bananas or greens especially if you drink lots of smoothies or green juice, like I do.

2. See if local neighbors, family or friends will share the price of getting cases of certain foods. When you do this, you can go beyond your local grocery store and contact great places (which deliver nationally) such as Boxed Greens (BoxedGreens.com) or Diamond Organics (Diamond Organics.com). Maybe they'll extend a discount if your order goes above a certain amount or if you get certain foods by the case. It never hurts to ask.

3. Pay attention to organic foods that are not very expensive to buy relative to the conventional prices (bananas, for example). Load up on those.

4. Be smart when picking what you buy as organic. Some

conventionally grown foods have higher levels of pesticides than others. For those, go organic. Then, for foods that are not sprayed as much, you can go conventional. Avocados, for example, aren't sprayed too heavily so you could buy those as conventional. Here is a resource that keeps an updated list: foodnews.org/walletguide.php

5. Buy produce that is on sale. Pay attention to which organic foods are on sale for the week and plan your menu around that. Every little bit adds up!

6. Grow your own sprouts. Load up on these for salads, soups, and smoothies. Very inexpensive. Buy the organic seeds in the bulk bins at your health food store or buy online and grow them yourself. Fun!

7. Buy organic seeds/nuts in bulk online and freeze. Nuts and seeds typically get less expensive when you order in bulk from somewhere like Sun Organic (SunOrganic.com). Take advantage of this and freeze them (they'll last the year!). Do the same with dried fruits/dates/etc. And remember, when you make a recipe that calls for expensive nuts, you can often easily replace them with a less expensive seed such as sunflower or pumpkin seeds.

8. Buy seasonally; hence, don't buy a bunch of organic berries out of season (i.e., eat more apples and bananas in the fall and winter). Also, consider buying frozen organic fruits, especially when they're on sale!

9. Be content with minimal variety from time to time. Organic spinach banana smoothies are inexpensive. You can change it up for fun by adding cinnamon one day, nutmeg another, vanilla extract yet another. Another inexpensive meal or snack is a spinach apple smoothie. Throw in

a date or some raisins for extra pizazz. It helps the budget when you make salads, smoothies, and soups with ingredients that tend to be less expensive such as carrots (year round), bananas (year round), zucchini and cucumbers (in the summer), etc.

Kristen Suzanne's Tip: A Note About Herbs

Hands down, fresh herbs taste the best and have the highest nutritional value. While I recommend fresh herbs whenever possible, you can substitute dried herbs if necessary. But do so in a ratio of:

3 parts fresh to 1 part dried

Dried herbs impart a more concentrated flavor, which is why you need less of them. For instance, if your recipe calls for three tablespoons of fresh basil, you'll be fine if you use one tablespoon of dried basil instead.

The Infamous Salt Question: What Kind Do I Use?

All life on earth began in the oceans, so it's no surprise that organisms' cellular fluids chemically resemble sea water. Saltwater in the ocean is "salty" due to many, many minerals, not just sodium chloride. We need these minerals, not coincidentally, in roughly the same proportion that they exist in... guess where?... the ocean! (You've just gotta love Mother Nature.)

So when preparing food, I always use sea salt, which can be found at any health food store. Better still is sea salt that was deposited into salt beds before the industrial revolution started spewing toxins into the world's waterways. My personal preference is Himalayan Crystal Salt, fine granules. It's mined high in the mountains from ancient sea-beds, has a beautiful pink color, and imparts more than 84 essential minerals into your diet. You can use either the Himalayan crystal variety or Celtic Sea Salt, but I would highly recommend sticking to at least one of these two. You can buy Himalayan crystal salt through KristensRaw .com/store.

Kristen Suzanne's Tip: Start Small with Strong Flavors

FLAVORS AND THEIR STRENGTH

There are certain flavors and ingredients that are particularly strong, such as garlic, ginger, onion, and salt. It's important to observe patience here, as these are flavors that can be loved or considered offensive, depending on who is eating the food. I know people who want the maximum amount of salt called for in a recipe and I know some who are highly sensitive to it. Therefore, to make the best possible Raw experience for you, I recommend starting on the "small end" especially with ingredients like garlic, ginger, strong savory herbs and seasonings, onions (any variety), citrus, and even salt. If I've given you a range in a recipe, for instance ¼–½ *teaspoon Himalayan crystal salt* then I recommend starting with the smaller amount, and then tasting it. If you don't love it, then add a little more of that ingredient and taste it again. Start small. It's worth the extra 60 seconds it might take you to do this. You might end up using less, saving it for the next recipe you make and voila, you're saving a little money.

LESSON #1: It's very hard to correct any flavors of excess, so start small and build.

LESSON #2: *Write it down.* When an ingredient offers a "range" for itself, write down the amount you liked best. If you use an "optional" ingredient, make a note about that as well.

One more thing to know about some strong flavors like the ones mentioned above… with Raw food, these flavors can intensify the finished product as each day passes. For example, the garlic in your soup, on the day you made it, might be perfect. On day two, it's still really great but a little stronger in flavor. And by day three, you might want to carry around your toothbrush or a little chewing gum!

HERE IS A TIP TO HELP CONTROL THIS

If you're making a recipe in advance, such as a dressing or soup that you won't be eating until the following day or even the day after that, then hold off on adding some of the strong seasonings until the day you eat it (think garlic and ginger). Or, if you're going to make the dressing or soup in advance, use less of the strong seasoning, knowing that it might intensify on its own by the time you eat it. This isn't a huge deal because it doesn't change that dramatically, but I mention it so you won't be surprised, especially when serving a favorite dish to others.

Kristen Suzanne's Tip: Doubling Recipes

More often than not, there are certain ingredients and flavors that you don't typically double in their entirety, if you're making a double or triple batch of a recipe. These are strong-flavored ingredients similar to those mentioned above (salt, garlic, ginger, herbs, seasoning, etc). A good rule of thumb is this: For a double batch, use 1.5 times the amount for certain ingredients. Taste it and see if you need the rest. For instance, if I'm making a "double batch" of soup, and the normal recipe calls for 1 tablespoon of Himalayan crystal salt, then I'll put in 1 ½ tablespoons to start, instead of two. Then, I'll taste it and add the remaining ½ tablespoon, if necessary.

This same principle is not necessarily followed when dividing a recipe in half. Go ahead and simply divide in half, or by whatever amount you're making. If there is a range for a particular ingredient provided, I still recommend that you use the smaller amount of an ingredient when dividing. Taste the final product and then decide whether or not to add more.

My recipes provide a variety of yields, as you'll see below. Some recipes make 2 servings and some make 4–6 servings. For those of you making food for only yourself, then simply cut the recipes making 4–6 servings in half. Or, as I always do... I make the larger serving size and then I have enough food for a couple of meals. If a recipe yields 2 servings, I usually double it for the same reason.

Kristen Suzanne's Tip: Changing Produce

"But I made it exactly like this last time! Why doesn't it taste the same?"

Here is something you need to embrace when preparing Raw vegan food. Fresh produce can vary in its composition of water, and even flavor, to some degree. There are times I've made marinara sauce and, to me, it was the perfect level of sweetness in the finished product. Then, the next time I made it, you would have thought I added a smidge of sweetener. This is due to the fact that fresh Raw produce can have a slightly different taste from time to time when you make a recipe (only ever so slightly, so don't be alarmed). *Aahhh, here is the silver lining!* This means you'll never get bored living the Raw vegan lifestyle because your recipes can change a little in flavor from time to time, even though you followed the same recipe. Embrace this natural aspect of produce and love it for everything that it is.

This is much less of an issue with cooked food. Most of the water is taken out of cooked food, so you typically get the same flavors and experience each and every time. Boring!

Kristen Suzanne's Tip: Ripeness and Storage for Your Fresh Produce

1. I never use green bell peppers because they are not "ripe." This is why so many people have a hard time digesting them (often "belching" after eating them). To truly experience the greatest health, it's important to eat fruits and vegetables at their peak ripeness. Therefore, make sure you only use red, orange, or yellow bell peppers. Store these in your refrigerator.

2. A truly ripe banana has some brown freckles or spots on the peel. This is when you're supposed to eat a banana. Store these on your countertop away from other produce, because bananas give off a gas as they ripen, which will affect the ripening process of your other produce. And, if you have a lot of bananas, split them up. This will help prevent all of your bananas from ripening at once.

3. Keep avocados on the counter until they reach ripeness (when their skin is usually brown in color and if you gently squeeze it, it "gives" just a little). At this point, you can put them in the refrigerator where they'll last up to a week longer. If you keep ripe avocados on the counter, they'll only last another couple of days. Avocados, like bananas, give off a gas as they ripen, which will affect the ripening process of your other produce. Let them ripen away from your other produce. And, if you have a lot of avocados, separate them. This will help prevent all of your avocados from ripening at once.

4. Tomatoes are best stored on your counter. Do not put them in the refrigerator or they'll get a "mealy" texture.

5. Pineapple is ripe for eating when you can gently pull a leaf out of the top of it. Therefore, test your pineapple for ripeness at the store to ensure you're buying the sweetest one possible. Just pull one of the leaves out from the top. After 3 to 4 attempts on different leaves, if you can't gently take one of them out, then move on to another pineapple.

6. Stone fruits (fruits with pits, such as peaches, plums, and nectarines), bananas and avocados all continue to ripen after being picked.

7. I have produce ripening all over my house. Sounds silly maybe, but I don't want it crowded on my kitchen countertop. I move it around and turn it over daily.

For a more complete list of produce ripening tips, check out my book, *Kristen's Raw*, available at Amazon.com.

Kristen Suzanne's Tip: Proper Dehydration Techniques

Dehydrating your Raw vegan food at a low temperature is a technique that warms and dries the food while preserving its nutritional integrity. When using a dehydrator, it is recommended that you begin the dehydrating process at a temperature of 130–140 degrees F for about an hour. Then, lower the temperature to 105 degrees F for the remaining time of dehydration. Using a high temperature such as 140 degrees F, *in the initial stages of dehydration*, does not destroy the nutritional value of the food. During this initial phase, the food does the most "sweating" (releasing moisture), which cools the food. Therefore, while the temperature of the air circulating *around* the food is about 140 degrees F, the food itself is much cooler. These directions apply only when using an Excalibur Dehydrator because of their Horizontal-Airflow Drying System. Furthermore, I am happy to only recommend Excalibur dehydrators because of their first-class products and customer service. For details, visit the *Raw Kitchen Essential Tools* section of my website at KristensRaw.com/store.

MY YIELD AND SERVING AMOUNTS NOTED IN THE RECIPES

Each recipe in this book shows an approximate amount that the recipe yields (the quantity it makes). I find that "one serving" to me might be considered two servings to someone else, or vice versa. Therefore, I tried to use an "average" when listing the serving amount. Don't let that stop you from eating a two-serving dish in one sitting, if it seems like the right amount for you. It simply depends on how hungry you are.

WHAT IS THE DIFFERENCE BETWEEN CHOPPED, DICED, AND MINCED?

Chop

Chopping gives relatively uniform cuts, but doesn't need to be perfectly neat or even. You'll often be asked to chop something before putting it into a blender or food processor, which is why it doesn't have to be uniform size since it'll be getting blended or pureed.

Dice

This produces a nice cube shape, and can be different sizes, depending on which you prefer. This is great for vegetables.

Mince

This produces an even, very fine cut, typically used for fresh herbs, onions, garlic and ginger.

Julienne

This is a fancy term for long, rectangular cuts.

WHAT EQUIPMENT DO I NEED FOR MY NEW RAW FOOD KITCHEN?

I go into much more detail regarding the perfect setup for your Raw vegan kitchen in my book, *Kristen's Raw,* which is a must read for anybody who wants to learn the easy ways to succeed with living the Raw vegan lifestyle. Here are the main pieces of equipment you'll want to get you going:

1. An excellent chef's knife (6–8 inches in length—non-serrated). Of everything you do with Raw food, you'll be chopping and cutting the most, so invest in a great knife. This truly makes doing all the chopping really fun!

2. Blender

3. Food Processor (get a 7 or 10-cup or more)

4. Juicer

5. Spiralizer or Turning Slicer

6. Dehydrator—Excalibur® is the best company by far and is available at KristensRaw.com

7. Salad spinner

8. Other knives (paring, serrated)

For links to online retailers that sell my favorite kitchen tools and foods, visit KristensRaw.com/store.

SOAKING AND DEHYDRATING NUTS AND SEEDS

This is an important topic. When using nuts and seeds in Raw vegan foods, you'll find that recipes sometimes call for them to be "soaked" or "soaked and dehydrated." Here is the low-down on the importance and the difference between the two.

Why Should You Soak Your Nuts and Seeds?

Most nuts and seeds come packed by Mother Nature with enzyme inhibitors, rendering them harder to digest. These inhibitors essentially shut down the nuts' and seeds' metabolic activity, rendering them dormant—for as long as they need to be—until they detect a moisture-rich environment that's suitable for germination (e.g., rain). By soaking your nuts and seeds, you trick the nuts into "waking up," shutting off the inhibitors so that the enzymes can become active. This greatly enhances the nuts' digestibility for you and is highly recommended if you want to experience Raw vegan food in the healthiest way possible.

Even though you'll want to soak the nuts to activate their enzymes, before using them, you'll need to re-dry them and grind them down anywhere from coarse to fine (into a powder almost like flour), depending on the recipe. To dry them, you'll need a dehydrator. (If you don't own a dehydrator yet, then, if a recipe calls for "soaked and dehydrated," just skip the soaking part; you can use the nuts or seeds in the dry form that you bought them).

Drying your nuts (but not yet grinding them) is a great thing to do before storing them in the freezer or refrigerator (preferably in glass mason jars). They will last a long time and you'll always have them on hand, ready to use.

In my recipes, I use nuts and seeds that are "soaked and de-hydrated" (that is, dry) unless otherwise stated in the directions as needing to be soaked (wet).

Some nuts and seeds don't have to follow the enzyme inhibitor rule; therefore, they don't need to be soaked. These are:

- Macadamia nuts
- Brazil nuts
- Pine nuts
- Hemp seeds
- Most cashews

An additional note... there are times when the recipe will call for soaking, even though it's for a type of nut or seed without en-zyme inhibitors, such as Brazil nuts. The logic behind this is to help *soften* the nuts so they blend into a smoother texture, es-pecially if you don't have a high-powered blender. This is helpful when making nut milks, soups and sauces.

Instructions for "Soaking" and "Soaking and Dehydrating" Nuts

"SOAKING"

The general rule to follow: Any nuts or seeds that require soak-ing can be soaked overnight (6–10 hours). Put the required amount of nuts or seeds into a bowl and add enough water to cover by about an inch or so. Set them on your counter over-night. The following morning, or 6–10 hours after you soaked them, drain and rinse them. They are now ready to eat or use in a recipe. At this point, they need to be refrigerated in an airtight container (preferably a glass mason jar) and they'll have a shelf life of about 3 days maximum. Only soak the amount you're going to need or eat, unless you plan on dehydrating them right away.

A note about flax seeds and chia seeds... these don't need to be soaked if your recipe calls for grinding them into a powder. Some recipes will call to soak the seeds in their "whole-seed" form, before making crackers and bread, because they create a very gelatinous and binding texture when soaked. You can soak flax or chia seeds in a ratio of one-part seeds to two-parts water, and they can be soaked for as short as 1 hour and up to 12 hours. At this point, they are ready to use (don't drain them). Personally, when I use flax seeds, I usually grind them and don't soak them. It's hard for your body to digest "whole" flax seeds, even if they are soaked. It's much easier for your body to assimilate the nutrients when they're ground to a flax meal.

"SOAKING AND DEHYDRATING"

Follow the same directions for soaking. Then, after draining and rinsing the nuts, spread them out on a mesh dehydrator sheet and dehydrate them at 140 degrees F for one hour. Lower the temperature to 105 degrees F and dehydrate them until they're completely dry, which can take up to 24 hours.

Please note, all nuts and seeds called for in my recipes will always be "Raw and Organic" and "Soaked and Dehydrated" unless the recipe calls for soaking.

ALMOND PULP

Some of my recipes call for "almond pulp," which is really easy to make. After making your fresh almond milk (see Nut/Seed Milk recipe, Appendix A) and straining it through a "nut milk bag," (available at NaturalZing.com or you can use a paint strainer bag from the hardware store—much cheaper), you will find a nice, soft pulp inside the bag. Turn the bag inside out and flatten the pulp out onto a ParaFlexx dehydrator sheet with a spatula or your hand. Dehydrate the pulp at 140 degrees F for one hour, then lower the temperature to 105 degrees F and continue dehydrating until the almond pulp is dry (up to 24 hours). Break the pulp into chunks and store in the freezer until you're ready to use it. Before using the almond pulp, grind it into a flour in your blender or food processor.

SOY LECITHIN

Some recipes (desserts, in particular) will call for soy lecithin, which is extracted from soybean oil. This optional ingredient is not Raw. If you use soy lecithin, I highly recommend using a brand that is "non-GMO," meaning it was processed without any genetically modified ingredients (a great brand is Health Alliance®). Soy lecithin helps your dessert (cheesecake, for example) maintain a firmer texture.

There is another lecithin option on the market, Sunflower Lecithin. This is used as an emulsifier in recipes. Soy lecithin is a common "go-to" source, but not everyone wants a soy product. That's all changed now that sunflower lecithin is available. You can find a link to purchase it at KristensRaw.com/store.

ICE CREAM FLAVORINGS

When making Raw vegan ice cream, it's better to use alcohol-free extracts so they freeze better.

SWEETENERS

The following is a list of sweeteners that you might see used in my recipes. It's important to know that the healthiest sweeteners are fresh whole fruits, including fresh dates. That said, dates sometimes compromise texture in recipes. As a chef, I look for great texture, and as a health food advocate, I lean towards fresh dates. But as a consultant helping people embrace a Raw vegan lifestyle, I'm also supportive of helping them transition, which sometimes means using raw agave nectar, or some other easy-to-use sweetener that might not have the healthiest ranking in the Raw food world, but is still much healthier than most sweeteners used in the Standard American Diet.

Most of my recipes can use pitted dates in place of raw agave nectar. There is some debate among Raw food enthusiasts as to whether agave nectar is Raw. The company I primarily use (Madhava®) claims to be Raw and says they do not heat their Raw agave nectar above 118 degrees F. If however, you still want to eat the healthiest of sweeteners, then bypass the raw agave nectar and use pitted dates. In most recipes, you can simply substitute 1–2 pitted dates for 1 tablespoon of raw agave nectar. Dates will not give you a super creamy texture, but the texture can be improved by making a "date paste" (pureeing pitted and soaked dates—with their soak water, plus some additional water, if necessary—in a food processor fitted with the "S" blade). This, of course, takes a little extra time.

If using raw agave nectar is easier and faster for you, then go ahead and use it; just be sure to buy the raw version that says they don't heat the agave above 118 degrees F. And, again, if you're looking to go as far as you can on the spectrum of health, then I recommend using pitted dates. Many of my recipes use raw agave nectar because that is most convenient for people.

Raw Agave Nectar

There are a variety of agave nectars on the market, but again, not all of them are Raw. Make sure it is labeled "Raw" on the bottle *as well as claiming that it isn't processed above 118 degrees F.* Just because the label says "Raw" does not necessarily mean it is so… do a double check and make sure it also claims "not to be heated above 118 degrees F." Agave nectar is noteworthy for having a low glycemic index.

Dates

Dates are probably the healthiest of sweeteners, because they're a fresh whole food (I'm a big fan of Medjool dates). Fresh organic dates are filled with nutrition, including calcium and magnesium. I like to call dates, "Nature's Candy."

Feel free to use dates instead of agave or honey in raw vegan recipes. If a recipe calls for ½ cup of raw agave, then you can substitute with approximately ½ cup of pitted dates (or more).

You can also make a recipe of Date Paste to replace raw agave (or to use in combination with it). It's not always as sweet as agave, so you might want to adjust the amount according to your taste by using a bit more Date Paste (see recipe, Appendix A).

Honey

Most honey is technically raw, but it is not vegan by most definitions of "vegan" because it is produced by animals, who therefore are at risk of being mistreated. While honey does not have the health risks associated with animal byproducts such as eggs or dairy, it can spike the body's natural sugar levels. Agave nectar has a lower, healthier glycemic index and can replace any recipe you find that calls for honey, in a 1 to 1 ratio.

Maple Syrup

Maple syrup is made from boiled sap of the maple tree. It is not considered raw, but some people still use it as a sweetener in certain dishes.

Rapadura®

This is a dried sugarcane juice, and it's not raw. It is, however, an unrefined and unbleached organic whole-cane sugar. It imparts a nice deep sweetness to your recipes, even if you only use a little. Feel free to omit it if you'd like to adhere to a strictly Raw program.

Stevia

This is from the leaf of the stevia plant. It has a sweet taste and doesn't elevate blood sugar levels. It's very sweet, so you'll want to use much less stevia than you would any other sweetener. My mom actually grows her own stevia. It's a great addition in fresh smoothies, for example, to add some sweetness without the calories. When possible, the best way to have stevia is grow it yourself.

Yacon Syrup

This sweetener has a low glycemic index, making it very attractive to some people. It has a molasses-type flavor that is very enjoyable. You can replace raw agave with this sweetener, but keep in mind that it's not as sweet in flavor as raw agave nectar. The brand I usually buy is Navitas Naturals, which is available at NavitasNaturals.com. For more information, see Appendix B, Resources.

SUN-DRIED TOMATOES

By far, the best sun-dried tomatoes are those you make yourself with a dehydrator. If you don't have a dehydrator, make sure you buy the "dry" sun-dried tomatoes, usually found in the bulk section of your health food market. Don't buy the kind that are packed in a jar of oil.

Also... don't buy sun-dried tomatoes if they're really dark (almost black) because these just don't taste as good. Again, I recommend making them yourself if you truly want the freshest flavor possible. It's really fun to do!

EATING WITH YOUR EYES

Most of us, if not all, naturally eat with our eyes before taking a bite of food. So, do yourself a favor and make your eating experience the best ever with the help of a simple, gorgeous presentation. Think of it this way, with real estate, it's always *location, location, location*, right? Well, with food, it's always *presentation, presentation, presentation*.

Luckily, Raw food does this on its own with all of its naturally vibrant and bright colors. But I take it even one step farther—I use my best dishes when I eat. I use my beautiful wine glasses for my smoothies and juices. I use my fancy goblets for many of my desserts. Why? Because I'm worth it. And, so are you! Don't save your good china just for company. Believe me, you'll notice the difference. Eating well is an attitude, and when you take care of yourself, your body will respond in kind.

ONLINE RESOURCES FOR GREAT PRODUCTS

For a complete and detailed list of my favorite kitchen tools, products, and various foods (all available online), please visit: KristensRaw.com/store.

BOOK & DVD RECOMMENDATIONS

I highly recommend reading the following life-changing books and DVDs.

- *Diet for a New America*, by John Robbins
- *The Food Revolution*, by John Robbins
- *The China Study*, by T. Colin Campbell
- *Skinny Bitch*, by Rory Freedman
- *Food, Inc.* (DVD)
- *Food Matters* (DVD)
- *The Future of Food* (DVD)
- *Earthlings* (DVD)

MEASUREMENT CONVERSIONS

1 tablespoon = 3 teaspoons

1 ounce = 2 tablespoons

¼ cup = 4 tablespoons

⅓ cup = 5 ⅓ tablespoons

1 cup = 8 ounces

= 16 tablespoons

= ½ pint

½ quart = 1 pint

= 2 cups

1 gallon = 4 quarts

= 8 pints

= 16 cups

= 128 ounces

Nourishing Rejuvelac

Yield 1 gallon

Rejuvelac is a cheesy-tasting liquid that is rich in enzymes and healthy flora to support a healthy intestine and digestion. Get comfortable making this super easy recipe because its use goes beyond just drinking it between meals.

Some people are concerned about the wheat aspect to wheat berries being used in most Rejuvelac recipes. While many people easily tolerate Rejuvelac made with wheat berries in spite of having wheat intolerance issues, there are other ingredients you can use to make Rejuvelac wheat-free. Some options are buckwheat, rice, quinoa, and more.

1 cup soft wheat berries, rye berries, or a mixture
water

Place the wheat berries in a half-gallon jar and fill the jar with water. Screw the lid on the jar and soak the wheat berries overnight (10–12 hours) on your counter. The next morning, drain and rinse them. Sprout the wheat berries for 2 days, draining and rinsing 1–2 times a day.

Then, fill the jar with purified water and screw on the lid, or cover with cheesecloth secured with a rubber band. Allow to ferment for 24–36 hours, or until the desired tartness is achieved. It should have a cheesy, almost tart/lemony flavor and scent.

Strain your rejuvelac into another glass jar and store in the refrigerator for up to 5–7 days. For a second batch using the same sprouted wheat berries, fill the same jar of already sprouted berries with water again, and allow to ferment for 24 hours. Strain off the rejuvelac as you did the time before this. You can do this process yet again, noting that each time the rejuvelac gets a little weaker in flavor.

Enjoy ¼–1 cup of Nourishing Rejuvelac first thing in the morning and/or between meals. It's best to start with a small amount and work your way up as your body adjusts.

Suggestion:

- For extra nutrition and incredible flavor, Nourishing Rejuvelac can be used in various recipes such as raw vegan cheeses, desserts, smoothies, soups, dressings and more. Simply use it in place of the water required by the recipe.

Date Paste

Yield 1–1 ¼ cups

It's great to keep this on hand in the refrigerator so you have it available and ready to use. Date Paste is easy to make and should take you less than 10 minutes to prepare once your dates are soaked. Store it in an airtight container in the refrigerator (a glass mason jar is perfect).

> **15 medjool dates, pitted, soaked 15 minutes (reserve soak water)**
>
> **¼–½ cup reserved "soak water"**

Using a food processor, fitted with the "S" blade, puree the ingredients until you have a smooth paste.

Crème Fraiche

Yield approximately 2 cups

1 cup raw cashews

¼–½ cup Nourishing Rejuvelac (see recipe, Appendix A)

1–2 tablespoons raw agave nectar

Place the cashews in a bowl and cover with enough water by about an inch. Let them soak for 1 hour. Drain off the water and give them a quick rinse.

Blend the ingredients until smooth. Store in an airtight glass mason jar for up to 5 days. This freezes well, so feel free to make a double batch for future use.

Nut/Seed Milk (regular)

Yield 4–5 cups

The creamiest nut/seed milk traditionally comes from hemp seeds, cashews, pine nuts, Brazil nuts or macadamia nuts, although I'm also a huge fan of milks made from walnuts, pecans, hazelnuts, almonds, sesame seeds, sunflower seeds, and pumpkin seeds.

This recipe does not include a sweetener, but when I'm in the mood for a little sweetness, I add a couple of pitted dates or a squirt of raw agave nectar. Yum!

1 ½ cups raw nuts or seeds

3 ¼ cups water

pinch Himalayan crystal salt, optional

Place the nuts in a bowl and cover with enough water by about an inch. Let them soak for 6-8 hours (unless you're using cashews, pine nuts, Brazil nuts, or macadamia nuts, in which case you only have to soak them about an hour. Hemp seeds do not need soaking because they're very soft and easy to blend, but adjust the amount of water used in the recipe, as needed). Drain off the water and give them a quick rinse.

Blend the ingredients until smooth and deliciously creamy. For an even *extra creamy* texture, strain your nut/seed milk through a nut milk bag.

Sweet Nut/Seed Cream (thick)

Yield 2–3 cups

1 cup raw nuts or seeds

1–1 ½ cups water, more if needed

2–3 tablespoons raw agave nectar or 3–4 dates, pitted

½ teaspoon vanilla extract, optional

Place the nuts in a bowl and cover with enough water by about an inch. Let them soak for 6–8 hours (unless you're using cashews, pine nuts, Brazil nuts, or macadamia nuts, in which case you only have to soak them about an hour. Hemp seeds do not need soaking because they're very soft and easy to blend, but adjust the amount of water used in the recipe, as needed). Drain off the water and give them a quick rinse.

Blend all of the ingredients until smooth.

Raw Mustard

2 teaspoons yellow mustard seeds, soaked 1–2 hours, then drained

½ cup extra virgin olive oil or hemp oil

1 tablespoon dry mustard powder

1 tablespoon apple cider vinegar

1 tablespoon fresh lemon juice or lime juice

¼ cup raw agave nectar

½ teaspoon Himalayan crystal salt

¼ teaspoon turmeric

Blend all of the ingredients together until smooth. It might be very thick, so if you want, add some water or oil to help thin it out. Adding more oil will help reduce the "heat" if it's too spicy for your taste.

Variation:

- "Honey" Mustard Version: Add more raw agave nectar (until you reach the desired sweetness)

My Basic Raw Mayonnaise

Yield about 2 ½ cups

People tell me all the time how much they like this recipe.

- **1 cup raw cashews**
- **½ teaspoon paprika**
- **2 cloves garlic**
- **1 teaspoon onion powder**
- **3 tablespoons fresh lemon juice**
- **¼ cup extra virgin olive oil or hemp oil**
- **2 tablespoons parsley, chopped**
- **2 tablespoons water, if needed**

Place the cashews in a bowl and cover with enough water by about an inch. Let them soak for 1 hour. Drain off the water and give them a quick rinse.

Blend all of the ingredients, except the parsley, until creamy. Pulse in the parsley. My Basic Raw Mayonnaise will stay fresh for up to one week in the refrigerator.

Appendix B

• • • • • • • • • •

Resources

The resources listed in this appendix are mostly raw, but you will also see a few items that are not raw.

BANANAS (FROZEN)

To make frozen bananas, simply peel (ripe) bananas, place them in a baggie or container, and put them in the freezer. I like to use my FoodSaver®, because it keeps the bananas from getting ice crystals on them. Having frozen bananas in your freezer at all times is a smart move. They are fantastic in smoothies, and they make a deliciously fun raw ice cream (just throw them in the food processor and puree them into a soft serve, raw vegan ice cream).

BREAD (SPROUTED)

You can buy this at the health food store. A couple of my favorite brands are *Good for Life* and *Manna Organics*.

CACAO LIQUOR (RAW)

This is the result of whole cacao beans that have been peeled and cold-pressed, which forms a paste. I use this to make a number of raw chocolate recipes. It comes in a block form and I melt it into a thick liquid using my dehydrator (or you can use a double boiler). It's bitter so I add sweetener. This is available from NavitasNaturals.com

CACAO NIBS (RAW)

These are partially ground cacao beans. They can be used in a variety of ways from toppings to raw vegan ice cream or yogurt. They add texture to shakes and smoothies, and you can make raw chocolates with them. They are available from NavitasNaturals .com and other sources online.

CAROB (RAW)

A lot of the carob you find in the store is toasted. I like to use raw carob, which has a wonderful flavor (caramel-like) and can be used in many recipes such as smoothies, nut milks, desserts, and more. There is a link for raw carob at KristensRaw.com/store.

CHIA SEEDS

These are called the "Dieter's Dream Food." Chia seeds are praised for many things including their fantastic nutrient profile, which proudly boasts iron, boron, essential fatty acids, fiber, and more. Add to that the claims that they may improve heart health, reduce blood pressure, stabilize blood sugar, help people lose weight from giving them extra stamina, energy, and curbing hunger, and you might become a fan of these little guys, too. They're superstars in my book. You can find a link for them at KristensRaw.com/store.

CHOCOLATE (CACAO) POWDER (RAW)

This is formed after the whole cacao beans have been peeled and cold-pressed. Then, the cacao oil is extracted and a powder remains. I use this in many recipes from making raw chocolate desserts to smoothies to soups to dressings and more. This is available from NavitasNaturals.com and other sources online.

COCONUT AMINOS

This is a seasoning sauce that can be used in place of tamari and namo shoyu. Available from the company, Coconut Secret, it's raw, enzymatically alive, organic, gluten-free, and soy-free. For more details, check out CoconutSecret.com. It's also available at some Whole Foods Markets.

COCONUT BUTTER OR *COCONUT SPREAD*

Coconut butter is not to be confused with plain coconut oil. Coconut butter is actually the coconut oil and coconut meat together in one jar. This can be eaten by the spoonful and it can also be used in desserts, smoothies, spreads, and more. There are two companies that I buy this from: WildernessFamilyNaturals.com offers a product they call "Coconut Spread" while Artisana calls theirs coconut butter. You can find the Artisana Coconut Butter at many health food stores including Whole Foods Market.

To make coconut butter easier (i.e., softer) to use, consider warming it in a dehydrator (at a low temperature).

DIAYA™ CHEESE

This is an amazing vegan cheese (not raw) that is taking the vegan world by storm. If you know of someone who misses artery-clogging, animal based cheese, then turn them on to this. It's soy-free, dairy-free, gluten-free, corn-free, and preservative-free. You can read more details at DaiyaFoods.com. I buy it from Whole Foods Market.

GOLDENBERRIES

These are also known as Incan Berries or Cape Gooseberries. They are basically a little dried fruit similar in shape to a raisin, and golden in color. The first time I tried these, I immediately thought, *"Move over crappy sour patch kids, it's time for something way more delish and oh-so-healthy at the same time!"* Goldenberries will throw a party in your mouth. These are available at NavitasNaturals .com

GOJI BERRIES

These little ruby colored jewels (also known as wolfberries) are a mega popular superfood because of their amazing nutrient content. They have 18 amino acids, including the 8 essential amino acids. Plus, their antioxidants are through the roof! The taste is a cross between a dried cherry and dried cranberry. I enjoy them plain and used in various recipes. My favorite source for them is Navitas Naturals (they're also available at various health food stores), and there is a link for them at KristensRaw.com/store.

GREEN POWDER(S)

Green powders are chock-full of powerful raw and alkalizing nutrition. My favorites are *Health Force Nutritionals' Vitamineral Green* and *Amazing Grass' Wheat Grass Powder.* Health Force Nutritionals also makes a green powder for pets called *Green Mush.* You will find links to these products at KristensRaw.com/store.

HEMP FOODS

Hemp is commonly referred to as a "superfood" because of its amazing nutritional value. Its amino acid profile dominates with the 8 essential amino acids (10 if you're elderly or a baby), making it a vegetarian source of "complete" protein. Manitoba Harvest is my favorite source for hemp products. I use their hemp seeds, hemp butter, hemp protein powder and hemp oil to make many delicious raw vegan recipes.

HERBAMERE™

This is an alternative to plain salt. It is a blend of sea salt and 14 organic herbs. It's a nice change of pace from plain salt. This is available on Amazon.com, other websites, and in some health food stores.

LUCUMA POWDER

Lucuma is a fun ingredient that is popular with Raw fooders. NavitasNaturals.com offers lucuma as a whole food powder, which adds a lovely sweetness to recipes with a flavor that has been described as a cross between sweet potato and maple. I love using lucuma powder in various raw recipes for smoothies, ice cream, cheesecake, nut milk, cookies, brownies, and more. There are other online sources for lucuma powder as well.

MACA POWDER

Maca is a plant that is used as a root and medicinal herb. Many people claim it gives them tons of energy and increased stamina for exercise, long workdays, and even libido! Personally, I'm not a huge fan of maca's flavor (to me, it smells like feet and tastes accordingly—haha), but this is one of the most popular superfoods among Raw vegans (so many people love it!), and for good reason with its reputed benefits. (Did I mention libido?) There is a link for maca powder at KristensRaw.com/store.

MESQUITE POWDER

This comes in a powder form that offers nutrition with a smoky, malt-like, and caramel flavor. This is available from NavitasNaturals .com and other online sources.

MISO

My all-time favorite source of organic miso is South River Miso. It's the ONLY brand I use. They have so many amazing flavors (including soy-free varieties). Check them out at SouthRiver-Miso.com. Two of my favorite flavors are *Dandelion Leek* and *Garlic Red Pepper.* You can use other brands of light or dark miso in place of the fancier flavors I've used in these recipes, but South River Miso is amazing so I highly recommend it.

MULBERRIES

These are lightly sweet with a wonderful texture that makes it hard to stop eating them. I consider these delights a superfood because of their nutrient content, including a decent source of protein. They are available from NavitasNaturals.com.

NON-DAIRY (PLANT-BASED) MILK

There are plenty of plant-based milks available for purchase in various grocery stores. They are not raw, but they are vegan and many are available as organic, which I highly recommend. Here are some options: almond, hemp, rice, soy, hazelnut, oat, and coconut. Plus, there are different flavors within those varieties such as plain, vanilla, and chocolate.

NUT / SEED BUTTERS (RAW)

Raw nut butters can be bought at most health food stores or you can easily make your own (simply grind nuts with a dash of Himalayan crystal salt in a food processor, fitted with the "S" blade, until you get a nut or seed butter. You might choose to add a little olive oil to help facilitate the processing. This could take 3–8 minutes).

There are different varieties available such as hemp seed butter, almond butter, hazelnut butter, pecan butter, sunflower seed butter, pumpkin seed butter, cashew butter, walnut butter, macadamia nut butter, and more. Some excellent brands are *Living Tree Community, Rejuvenative Brands, Wilderness Poets (online)*, and *Artisana*. I usually buy them from Whole Foods Market.

OLIVES (RAW)

I truly love *Essential Living Foods'* Black Bojita Olives. They are juicy, fresh, and delicious. It's hard to stop at eating only one! They are available at Whole Foods Market and online at EssentialLivingFoods.com. I also use *Living Tree Community's* Sun-Dried Olives in some recipes. They're different in taste and texture than the Black Bojita Olives.

OLIVE OIL (RAW)

I enjoy two truly raw olive oils: *Living Tree Community* (LivingTreeCommunity.com, also available at some Whole Foods Markets) and *Wilderness Family Naturals* (available online at WildernessFamilyNaturals.com).

ORANGE PEEL POWDER

This is a powder, which is the dried, finely ground orange peel (it's where you'll find many of the orange's nutrients, too). This is available from MountainRoseHerbs.com (They also have lemon peel powder.)

PROTEIN POWDER

I use various raw vegan protein powders to get extra protein in my life. My favorites are hemp and sprouted raw brown rice protein powders.

In general, when I'm drinking the sprouted raw brown rice protein powder (by just mixing it with water), I like the chocolate and natural flavors from *Sun Warrior* or the plain flavor of *Sprout Living's EPIC Protein*. Hemp foods, *Sun Warrior* protein powder and *Sprout Living* protein powder are available at KristensRaw.com/store.

RAPADURA

This is a dried sugarcane juice, and it is not Raw. It is, however, an unrefined and unbleached organic whole-cane sugar. I buy mine at Whole Foods Market.

RIGHTEOUSLY RAW CACAO BARS (EARTH SOURCE ORGANICS)

Even though this is not an ingredient in which you'd use to make a recipe, I had to mention it here (it's an actual product for organic, raw, vegan chocolate bars). In my opinion, this is the best raw chocolate bar on the market. My favorite flavor is the Caramel Cacao but they also sell Goji, Maca, and Acai. Sometimes I just don't have time to make my own raw chocolate and sometimes I'm just plain lazy. In both cases, I run to Whole Foods Market for these (you can also buy them online direct from the company: earthsourceorganics.com). If your Whole Foods doesn't stock these... tell them to do it! Check out my blog post where I talked about my first encounter with these divine treats.

http://kristensraw.blogspot.com/2010/review-earth-source-organics.html

ROLLED OATS

I use traditional organic oats from SunOrganic.com or raw oats available at NaturalZing.com.

SAUERKRAUT (RAW, UNPASTEURIZED)

You can buy sauerkraut from the health food store or make it yourself (my favorite way). If you choose to buy it from the store, be sure to get a brand that is organic, raw, and unpasteurized. Two brands that I like are *Gold Mine Natural Foods* and *Rejuvenative Foods* (they're both great, but my overall preference is Gold Mine Natural Foods).

However, making your own is the best. It's incredibly easy and fun. For directions on making your own sauerkraut, please see my blog posts and video here:

http://kristensraw.blogspot.com/2009/07/how-to-make-sauerkraut-video-raw.html

SESAME OIL (RAW)

You can get this from RejuvenativeFoods.com.

STEVIA

Stevia is an all-natural sweetener from the stevia plant. It has a sweet taste and doesn't elevate blood sugar levels. It is very sweet, so you will want to use much less stevia than you would any other sweetener. I buy mine from Navitas Naturals (available at NavitasNaturals.com)

SUN-DRIED OLIVES

I buy the brand *Living Tree Community* at Whole Foods Market or online at LivingTreeCommunity.com.

SUNFLOWER LECITHIN

This is popular for its choline content, and it's also used as an emulsifier in recipes. Soy lecithin is a common "go-to" source for this purpose, but not everyone wants a soy product. That is all changed now that sunflower lecithin is available. I like adding it to raw soups, smoothies, desserts, and more. You can find a link for it at KristensRaw.com/store.

TEECCINO®

This is an alkaline herbal "coffee" (it's not really coffee) that my family loves since giving up regular coffee. It is available at many health food stores like Whole Foods Market. It's also available online (Amazon.com). For details about the awesomeness of this product, check out Teeccino.com.

VEGGIE BURGER

I LOVE Organic *Sunshine Burgers* veggie burgers, which I buy in the freezer department of Whole Foods Market. Check out their website at SunshineBurger.com.

WAKAME FLAKES

The wakame flakes that I use are from Navitas Naturals. Here is what they have to say about this particular product on their website at NavitasNaturals.com:

"One of the most hearty vegetables of the sea, wakame is in fact an algae that is amongst the oldest living species on Earth. This sea green has been used extensively in traditional Japanese, Chinese, and Korean cuisine as an important health food and key component of Eastern medicine for centuries. Wakame is a balanced combination of essential organic minerals including iron, calcium, and magnesium, alongside valuable trace minerals as well. Additionally, wakame is well known for its detoxifying antioxidants, Omega 3 fatty acids (in the form of Eicospentaenoic acid), and body-building vegetable proteins. Wakame also provides many vitamins like vitamin C and much of the B spectrum, and serves as an excellent source of both soluble and insoluble fiber."

Impressive, huh?

WHEAT GRASS POWDER

I use Amazing Grass' Wheat Grass Powder available at KristensRaw.com/store.

YACON SYRUP, POWDER, AND SLICES

This is an alternative sweetener offering a low glycemic index so it's commonly viewed as diabetic friendly. According to Navitas-Naturals.com (the brand I prefer for yacon products), *"... yacon tastes sweet, the sugar of inulin is not digestible and simply passes through the body. Therefore, yacon only contains about half the calories of an average sugar source. Secondly, FOS (promotes the production of healthy probiotics within the body, which can contribute to better digestion and colon health."*

As a reader of this book, you are entitled to a 10% discount off Excalibur dehydrators and products:

CPSIA information can be obtained
at www.ICGtesting.com
Printed in the USA
BVHW081354010619
549887BV00002B/271/P